This book is the first to provide English readers with a brief and comprehensive survey of economic life in Italy during the period of its greatest splendour: the Middle Ages and Renaissance. The wealth of Renaissance Italy was the product of centuries of growth, and the great Renaissance cities, Venice, Milan and Florence, were first and foremost centres of international trade, which taught the rest of Europe the rudiments of modern business techniques. In a masterly synthesis, based upon a lifetime of study and research, Professor Gino Luzzatto, the greatest of living Italian historians, describes the main changes in Italian economic conditions from the end of the Roman Empire, when Italy ceased to be the centre of a European state, to the end of the Middle Ages when Italy lost the leadership of European trade and banking. The narrative chapters, which deal with barbarian Italy, feudal Italy and Italy in the age of the communes, are followed by a valuable analysis of medieval agriculture, industry, commerce and finance, in her principal Italian states. The range of discussion is wide and offers an excellent introduction to the economic history not only of Italy but of the whole Mediterranean region.

AN ECONOMIC HISTORY OF
ITALY

AN ECONOMIC HISTORY OF
ITALY

from the Fall of the Roman Empire
to the beginning of
the Sixteenth Century

GINO LUZZATTO

Translated from the Italian
by Philip Jones

52397

NEW YORK
BARNES & NOBLE, INC.

First published
in the United States of America
1961

© *Routledge & Kegan Paul Limited 1961*

Printed in Great Britain

Contents

Contents

Contents

CHAPTER ONE

The Last Two Centuries
of the Western Empire

I. STRUCTURAL CHANGES IN THE EMPIRE DURING ITS
FIRST 250 YEARS AND THEIR ECONOMIC EFFECTS

THE economic condition of Italy during the first five centuries of the Middle Ages was powerfully influenced by structural changes in the late Roman Empire and the effect they produced on Rome and Italy generally. The peaceful centuries of the early Empire had been a period of widespread prosperity, which reached its peak in the reign of Trajan and his immediate successors. At that time was established the great network of highways, which served trade as much as government and defence, and by linking Rome with all corners of the Empire, made the city in every sense the centre of the civilized world. It was an age of energetic building, which saw the construction of many new and well-furnished ports, of canals and aqueducts, markets and inns, temples, theatres, and amphitheatres. The system of government also changed, and a constitution based on the ruling city, to which the provinces, though separate and partly autonomous, were uniformly subject, was steadily replaced by a unified Empire, centrally administered, by a vast bureaucracy with power extending over every province. In the words of a later writer, the whole world had become one city (*urbem fecisti quod prius orbis erat*). By the second century the language, law, and coinage of Rome were everywhere in use, and the Empire formed a single market, which all the provinces shared in perfect parity with Italy and Rome.

This was a great achievement, and its effects are still felt even today. At the time, however, the "Roman peace" brought problems as well as benefits. In particular it arrested the flow of war captives, which down to the last century B.C. had replenished the market for slaves. In Italy the number of slaves, which in Augustus's time is thought to have reached some two-fifths of the population, rapidly fell in the next two centuries, partly because of failing supplies, partly because the birth-rate was very much lower among slaves than among freemen. Attempts to remedy this by granting slaves the right to raise a family and acquire possessions (*peculium*) were of little effect; the decline continued and soon affected every phase of economic life. In the past, when slaves were cheap and plentiful, rich men had used their capital to establish large slave-run estates and factories; but after the reign of Augustus the growing scarcity and cost of slaves condemned large industry to disorganization and decay. Increasingly the great estates were parcelled out in farms let to peasants (*coloni*), either free peasants, freed slaves, or "hutted" slaves (*servi casati*) who had been granted a house and holding in return for fixed payments to the owner. But these new methods did not solve the problems of production. Tenants fell badly into arrears with payments, and at the turn of the first century so substantial a landlord as Pliny the Younger was quite unable to collect his rents. For this reason a mixed system was finally adopted both in Italy and the provinces; estates were divided into two parts, one being worked by the owner and the other distributed in holdings, let in most cases for a share of the crops and a small money rent. But as slaves were now too few to cultivate home farms unaided, the practice spread of making tenants also render services and work a number of days each year in the fields of the landlord. This system—which as we shall see was further developed and perfected in the early Middle Ages—might have restored some balance to the rural economy of Italy, had it been left to work undisturbed. But too many factors were against it. Most obvious was the growing financial pressure of the state, which made taxation insupportable to many classes of society. In addition to this Italian industry and agriculture were faced by increasing competition from the provinces. The population also began to decline, especially in peninsular Italy and the islands. In these conditions public morality steadily decayed, so that defence and even production were neglected.

Oppressive taxation was the consequence of territorial conquest, for only a paid professional army of soldiers and officials could administer the vast dominions of imperial Rome and defend its extensive frontiers against attack from Germans and Huns, Slavs and Persians. In the past, taxes had been levied only occasionally, to pay for wars or embassies or public works, and current expenditure had been met out of patrimonial revenue. But these methods were no longer enough. New and regular taxes had to be devised to cover the new regular expenses. Some of the taxes introduced were raised indirectly; but the most important and burdensome charge was a direct tax assessed on land and the people working it. This land tax not only reached the humblest members of the peasantry; it also imposed a double liability on the landowners, for the land in their possession and the taxes of their tenants.

2. COMPETITION FROM THE PROVINCES

Even more serious for Italy than fiscal rapacity were the economic consequences of imperial unification and the westward spread of techniques of production and organization which had first been perfected in the Graeco-Roman world. Recently an English historian has pointed out three distinct phases in this "Romanization" of the frontier provinces. To start with, inevitably, the army took charge, busily constructing forts, roads, and bridges, and even providing its own material from factories built and run by the soldiers themselves. Next, Italian merchants came on the scene, at first simply to supply the troops, and then to trade with the natives. In the third and final stage—which most concerns us here—the western provinces began to copy the products of Italian industry, learned to cultivate the main commercial products of Italian farming, such as wine and oil, and began trading on their own account. With this the economic primacy of Italy was broken. The newly Romanized dominions, Gaul and Spain especially, were now no longer subjects but rivals, drawing off demand from Italian goods not only locally in their own domestic markets, but also in neighbouring regions like western Germany and Britain. The clearest case of this was Gaul. Gallic potteries for instance

3

undermined irreparably the great ceramic industry of Arezzo, once the largest in the Empire, while Gallic glass and bronze ware competed sharply with Italian products, particularly in the trade with Germany. No less emphatic was the challenge from agriculture, the basic industry of Gaul in Roman times as now. Land was plentiful and fertile, and free farm labour easy to find; and so it only needed Roman methods of husbandry to produce large quantities of surplus crops for export, of grain, wine, and oil. Grain from the Loire valley and the rich plains of Gascony was sent as far as Ostia, the main port of Rome, and helped to feed the capital; the first travelled by way of the Saône and Rhône to Arles, the second by way of Narbonne. Grain from northern Gaul by contrast was shipped down the Scheldt and the Meuse to feed the armies of the Rhine. Wine and oil were large-scale products of the Midi. The wines of Provence indeed were already well known in the later years of the Republic. Even so, some two centuries probably elapsed before they interfered at all with the market for Italian vintages, the best of which remained in great demand all over Gaul. Only after A.D. 200 do we hear of Gaul exporting wine. The economic progress of Gaul was shared by the richest part of Spain, the province of Baetica, which also managed to grow enough corn and wine for export and still more olive oil. Excavations made at Rome into the enormous mound of potsherds known by the name of *Monte Testaccio* have disclosed a mass of *amphorae* said to total 40 millions, all coming from Baetica and most of them used for carrying oil. Since the capacity of every *amphora* was something like 11 gallons, this means that 440 million gallons of oil were shipped from Spain to Rome in the space of several decades.

One circumstance which fostered competition from the provinces was undoubtedly the high cost of transport, especially of bulky goods. At a time when an overland journey of less than 300 miles could double the price of a product such as hemp, countries such as Germany or Gaul which were favoured with excellent waterways were bound to profit greatly. The loss to Italy was correspondingly severe, though not perhaps so catastrophic as some historians like Rostovtzeff have supposed. The declining market for Italian manufactures, and still more Italian agricultural produce, certainly combined with other influences to bring increasing hardship on a number of Italian towns and on most parts of the Italian countryside. By causing prices to fall just when the scarcity and high cost of slaves and the mounting burden of taxation were driving many men to despair, provincial competition reduced the ancient industries in many towns to impotence or ruin, and made it quite profitless, in many country districts, to farm land responsibly or even at all.

3. DEPOPULATION AND DISAFFECTION

A further sign and consequence of these conditions was a decline in population, which, though most clearly proved in regard to the slave population, almost certainly affected society as a whole. Many Italians of free condition are known to have settled abroad. The prevailing tendency had been to drift into the towns, and this process went on unceasingly throughout the final century of the Republic and the first 150 years of the Empire, until Rome acquired a population of a million or more. But there were limits to what the towns could take or the government distribute in free food to necessitous citizens. For these an obvious way out was to "go west". Many of the soldiers and civilians, in fact, who were planted as official colonists in the provinces, had once been small proprietors back in Italy. Other migrants set off on their own, in the following of merchants, tax farmers, and officials, or simply to try their luck. They have left no record of their numbers, but they must have formed a very large company, if the Romanization of so many areas west of the Rhine and south of the Pyrenees was rapid and profound enough to survive all subsequent invasions of foreign peoples and customs.

The loss by immigration was intensified by a falling birthrate. Official records and literature both refer to this. As early as Augustus's reign alarm was expressed at the general "lack of young men" (*penuria juventutis*). Then, in Nero's reign, the poet Lucan complains of towns being deserted and fields abandoned for want of hands to till them. Many districts were desolated by malaria, known nowadays to be the effect rather than the cause of depopulation. The Tuscan Maremma and

5

Roman Campagna, the Pontine Marshes and Magna Graecia were all infested, yet all had once been populous and thriving. Under Tiberius and Nero, Samnium and much of Apulia were also falling waste, and even Campania, the most flourishing and densely-peopled part of the peninsula, was so far affected that the towns destroyed by Vesuvius (in A.D. 79) were never rebuilt. Somewhat later, we find the population of Rome itself in sharp decline: the daily corn requirement of the capital, assessed at about 40,000 bushels in the time of Augustus, had dropped to little more than 18,000 bushels by the time of Septimius Severus. Last to suffer was the Po valley, economically the most vigorous part of Italy, which down to the second century had probably supported a rising population. Some of the greater northern cities, like Milan and Pavia, Padua and Aquileia, retained conspicuous importance and even took the leading place among Italian towns during the later Empire. But others showed signs of decay: Este, for example, prosperous in Augustus's time, a century later was half deserted; by the early fourth century Vercelli and Bologna, Modena and Piacenza all contained wide ruined spaces within their walls.

Depopulation and decay were dismal enough effects of the changes occurring in the Empire; but perhaps most pernicious of all was the complete alienation of the people from the state. Once citizens were excluded from every share in public life and denied all influence even in local government, which was no longer granted independent power, the state simply assumed the character of tax-gatherer, extorting services and tribute, which men felt justified in using every means to escape. They dodged military service and they evaded municipal office, which was now much more a charge than an honour, and they even stopped producing as much as they might for fear that the government would reap more benefit from it than they did.

4. MILITARY AND MONETARY ANARCHY

The undiminished splendour of Rome in the mid third century and the manifest prosperity of many towns in Cisalpine Gaul, of Aquileia, and of certain provinces in east and west, could scarcely hide these various causes of weakness which were steadily destroying a mighty Empire. The disparity between the ruling country and its dependent provinces and the incompetence of Rome to maintain control over all parts of its dominion became increasingly obvious; and when Caracalla in 212 conferred rights of citizenship on all free men in the provinces, he was really making no great change, for citizenship was no longer of any importance, and provincials already dominated in fact all departments of the state—the army, the civil service, and even the imperial office itself. As the provinces grew in wealth and economic independence they resented more and more the burden of a costly capital. There was no attempt yet to break away, but local risings, mostly by the army, became so frequent in the later third century that the period is known as the "military anarchy".

The evils of civil war were made more intolerable by the heavy fiscal charges imposed by each pretender to the throne, in order to reward with increased pay the troops who had raised him to power. All kinds of arbitrary taxes and services were levied, sometimes from single towns, sometimes from professional groups, sometimes from mere individuals; and for these exactions the greater landlords of each locality were made to pledge their estates. Conditions reached their worst, it seems, during the dim period between the reign of Alexander Severus and that of Diocletian, when the country had to bear, besides all its other tribulations, a plundering attack by the Alemanni, the first barbarians to enter Italy since the Gauls, Cimbri, and Teutons centuries before.

One revealing symptom of the reckless increase in state expenditure and the general disorganization of trade was the progressive debasement of the imperial coinage, especially of silver. The gold coin, the *aureus*, was only twice debased: once by Nero, who reduced its weight from 8·18 to 7·4 grams, and then by Constantine, who issued a new gold coin, the *solidus*, with a weight of 4·55 grams, that remained constant thereafter in the Byzantine Empire until the twelfth century. Very different was the history of the silver *denarius*, which fell so far in value that a comprehensive tariff (*Edictum*) of maximum prices had to be published in 301 to combat the resulting inflation. Some decline was apparent in Trajan's reign, when the weight of the *denarius* was lowered from 3·9 to 3·21 grams; then, under Septimius Severus, the silver content sank to less than 2 grams, and under Caracalla, to as low as 1·5 per cent of the whole. This debased *denarius*, which was little better than silver-washed bronze, Septimius Severus and his successors tried to enforce by ordinance; yet so bad was the coin then being issued by the mints that the government itself would not accept it, and compelled all people to pay at least a part of their taxes in kind. Nor was this the only cause of grievance; for as always happens in times of acute monetary inflation, coin became scarce, and substitute forms of currency arose, tallies and coupons of various kinds, which made the chaos complete.

In these conditions of combined military and monetary anarchy the economy became more cruelly disrupted than ever: city after city was depopulated, and both town and country were afflicted by a general shortage of labour. In desperation the dangerous remedy was tried, first in the frontier districts and then nearer home, of introducing barbarians, some into the army, some on to the land, and some even as time went on into the highest offices of state.

In spite of all that has just been said it is still possible to overdo the picture of universal economic breakdown and barbarian menace to the frontiers of the late third-century Empire. Even during the very worst years of anarchy, labour did not cease altogether in the fields and workshops; some places escaped the wars and violence, and preserved unchanged the traditional forms of industrial and agricultural life. The inflation itself, severe though it was, never caused a complete return to a natural economy, and however debased in value, money did not wholly disappear. The markets went on, the cities continued to be centres of exchange, amid their evident decay, and town and country remained in close dependence and partnership. Even the writings of the Christian Fathers, which give a black enough account of things, betray the existence of a world only too familiar with transactions based on money: in the fourth and fifth centuries they still talk about rich men who lend out their cash through bankers, not only to people in immediate need, but also to men of business. It was not yet a world in total dissolution, but rather a society where all production and exchange had been paralysed by disorder and insecurity.

5. THE REORGANIZATION OF THE EMPIRE BY DIOCLETIAN AND CONSTANTINE; THE ORIENTAL DESPOTISM

It was just when the collapse of Roman civilization and institutions seemed most imminent that a succession of unusually able men ascended the imperial throne—Claudian, Aurelian, and above all Diocletian—who by their victories in arms drove back the danger of foreign invasion, and by their comprehensive reforms restored the fabric of the Empire for more than a century. Their first concern was to reassert the authority of the state, and this they did by adopting the methods and principles of eastern despotism and assuming outright control not only of the government, army, and administration, but also of economic life throughout the Empire. The economy was "bureaucratized", or rather, as an English historian has put it, using a term familiar in recent times, a "corporative Empire" was established. One means tried was the Edict of 301 already mentioned, by which Diocletian sought to check inflation and make goods cheap by fixing salaries and prices by decree. But, since he failed to stop the deterioration of money, prices and salaries continued to rise in defiance of the law. It was reserved for Constantine a few years later to induce some stability of circulation and moderate the rise in prices, by reducing the legal value of gold and still more of silver currency. More successful were the steps taken by Diocletian, and afterwards by Constantine, to make all economic activity subservient to the military and financial needs of the state, along lines already forecast in earlier centuries, especially in the Hellenistic east. The device used was to tie every man to his occupation and make it hereditary from father to son: the peasant might not quit his holding or turn to other employment, the artisan must stick for ever to his craft, and so on from class to class. This perpetual bond was even enforced on the holders of municipal office (*curiales*).

The purpose behind this immense labour of collective discipline and organization in state and society was primarily

The Last Two Centuries

financial. Compelled as it was to face increasing expenditure on frontier defences and the maintenance of order, on a vast bureaucracy and a lavish Oriental court, the government found that the best way to ensure the payment of taxes was to make them the corporate responsibility of groups or classes united by a common profession or occupation. At the same time this fiscal device provided a means of controlling the entire economy. For the Emperors were not content with the influence they exercised by the simple fact of owning more land than anyone else or acquiring more food and goods, for the purpose of supplying the capital, the court, and the army. Nor were they satisfied with the opportunity offered for interference by their monopoly of the coinage and the customs system. But they also decided to make an instrument out of the ancient guilds (*collegia*), voluntary charitable and religious institutions which the state now transformed into compulsory, monopolistic corporations. Compulsory membership of a guild, which in many cases was made hereditary, was limited at first to those trades and professions which served the government; but since most occupations were now largely tributary to the government, the final effect was to change the nature of the whole economy and supersede all free enterprise by strict state controls.

It is most unlikely that the reforms carried out by Diocletian and Constantine were inspired by any "ideology", though they were certainly influenced by the living tradition and examples of Oriental despotism. What drove these Emperors to develop such a severely centralized and restrictive system was not a set of abstract principles, but the compelling practical need to save the Empire from anarchy and invasion. And like the chains which keep old buildings from collapsing, the restraint they imposed probably did postpone the fall of the Empire for more than a century, and even allowed it some short moments of recovery. But this was only done at the cost of making complete and irreparable the divorce of the state from its subjects, which then deprived the Empire of the strength it needed when confronted, not long after, by the last mortal threat from the outside.

6. THE GERMANIC INVASIONS AND THE FALL OF THE
WESTERN EMPIRE

Less than fifty years after the death of Constantine barbarian
tribes began to threaten the frontiers again, overrunning border
areas like the lower Danube and organizing raids and even outright invasions far into imperial territory. The most devastating
attack came from the Visigoths who, under the leadership of
Alaric their king, crossed the eastern Alps into Italy, put Rome
itself to the sack, and then withdrew upon southern Gaul and
Spain. To halt the advance of the Germans who lived closest to
the frontier and were most influenced by contacts with Rome,
the Emperors chose the dubious expedient of planting whole
tribes of armed barbarians on Roman soil, which it was fondly
presumed they would then protect from attack by other migrant
invaders.

The disorder was increased by struggles inside the Empire
and by bitter outbreaks of religious dissension, which often
ended in bloodshed, violence, and pillage. But what did the
greatest harm, even in regions most exposed to barbarian in-
roads, spreading economic ruin far and wide, was still the
fiscal oppression of the state, now more burdensome than ever,
and the pitiless system of collective responsibility from which
no department of public and private life was exempt. Town
councillors or *curiales*, chosen from among the greater landowners, were made personally responsible for the tax charged
against their city; the guilds were liable for all the tax imposed
on crafts and industry; and landlords had to pay the tax-quota
due from neighbouring properties which had been abandoned
and were regarded by the state as forming one with their own.
Such fiscal methods could only extinguish all spirit of initiative
and destroy the will of many people to carry on production and
perform the public duties which, according to their social rank,
they were called upon to fulfil. Particularly severe in its effect
on husbandry was the practice, just mentioned, of transferring
the tax registered against vacant holdings as a surcharge upon
adjoining land. This simply penalized the diligent and hard-
working owner for his efforts to contend with a dangerous and
difficult position, and encouraged him to follow the example of

his less conscientious neighbour and escape from an intolerable and iniquitous imposition by taking flight.

It is true that the dismal accounts which survive of the state of western Europe about the end of the fourth century, and the stories of land increasingly abandoned and depopulated, are all the work of Christian authors, driven by religious passion and an uncompromising struggle with pagans and heretics to make things look as black as possible. But the laws of the time also describe in unambiguous language the relentless progress of depopulation, disorganization, and poverty. Sixty years after Constantine's death official records disclose 53,000 *iugera* of waterlogged land in Campania alone, as well as other land desolate from want of men to work it. Conditions were no better in Picenum, Samnium, Bruttium, and Apulia, all of which had to be excused arrears of taxation. In 413, following the Visigothic invasion, the Emperor Honorius was forced to reduce by one-fifth the taxes of Campania, Tuscia, Picenum, Samnium, Lucania, and Bruttium, and five years later he had to abate still more those of Campania, Tuscia, and Picenum.

It must be said that the decline was not uniform in all parts of the Empire, or even of Italy. Thus the new Rome, which Constantine had founded with prophetic insight on the shores of the Bosphorus, was able in the space of a few decades to challenge ancient Rome, not only in the splendour of its buildings but even more, thanks to a favoured position, in the vigour and vitality of its trade. To some extent certain towns of northern Italy, such as Milan and Aquileia, Padua and Ravenna, also continued to prosper in the first half of the fifth century. Milan, which for over a century, down to 404, replaced Rome as the seat of imperial government, grew conspicuously in population and supported many flourishing industries, especially in textiles and metalwork. It became the largest town in the valley of the Po, and was surpassed only by Aquileia, in the far north-eastern corner of the northern plain, which was another great centre of manufactures and of transalpine trade with the countries of the middle Danube. Ravenna was not so important economically, but its fortunate situation, close to the Adriatic coast and safely distant from the roads travelled by invading armies, caused its choice as the final capital of the western Empire in the fifth century, and as the capital of Byzantine

Italy for over two hundred years. This is why traces of the Roman guild system persist longer here than anywhere else.

The survival and relative prosperity of these and lesser towns prevented northern Italy and some parts of south and central Italy from suffering the same degree of social dislocation as other European countries, where numerous small and self-sufficient groups had grown up among the ruins of an economy formerly based on exchange. Over most of western Europe at this time life was coming to be organized round the manor houses and farms (*villae*) of the few rich and powerful landlords, whose influence was no longer limited to their own dependants, living scattered on their great estates, but was also extended under the name of protection to the free peasants gathered in the villages (*vici*). In this way local communities were founded, which in fact if not in law were largely autonomous and in production were often self-supporting; slave-run workshops were built near the villa and the great estate became itself a market for local trade in goods and services. In Italy, however, unlike Gaul or Britain, there is no clear proof that such self-sufficient *villae* ever existed. Some there may have been, but they must have been exceptional, because the numberless towns which survived, despite decay, even in the darkest years of the later Empire, kept alive the rudiments of an exchange economy which found its natural centre in the towns.

But if the dissolution of the old Roman world was never so complete in Italy, especially northern Italy, as it was elsewhere, the fact remains that the attempt at reconstruction by Diocletian and Constantine, while successful in the eastern provinces where it harmonized with ancient tradition, was utterly defeated in the west where totalitarian methods produced an effect quite unforeseen by the men who hoped they would bring salvation. When all refused to study or obey what was offered as the common interest, the system had manifestly failed.

CHAPTER TWO

From the Fall of the Western Empire to the Partition of Italy between Greeks and Lombards

1. ITALY UNDER THE OSTROGOTHS

NOWADAYS most historians agree that the barbarian invasions caused no deep or sudden break between the ancient and the medieval world, though they certainly hurried on the economic ruin of the western Empire. There is good reason to believe that in Italy, as in Gaul and in certain areas along the Rhine and the upper Danube, the effect of the invasions on the economic structure and institutions of the country was quite insignificant during the first 150 years after the deposition of Romulus Augustulus. During the brief rule of Odoacer (476–89), who was not an invader but the rebel leader of barbarian troops (Heruli, Rugians, Turcilingi) in the service of the Empire, not the slightest attempt was made to substitute a new order for the old. Odoacer did not take the title of king nor did he issue any laws of his own, like the codes of Romano-Germanic custom published in other barbarian states of western Europe. As for the Italians, they had long grown accustomed to seeing a barbarian rule in the name of an impotent Emperor, and they must have noticed little change in things, especially when Odoacer continued to choose his counsellors and ministers from the Roman aristocracy. The only possible cause of upheaval was the allocation of a third of all landed property to Odoacer's soldiers, who had first rebelled against Orestes to obtain this very thing. In practice the disturbance was probably slight. Land distributions were not unheard of before; on this occasion

14

the soldiers were relatively few, for they occupied only certain provinces, while land itself, whether imperial property or private property which had been abandoned, was available in plenty.

The first, or rather the only, Romano-Germanic kingdom founded on Italian soil, was the Ostrogothic kingdom which followed after Odoacer's short thirteen years of government. This again brought no violent rupture with the past, for the Goths had long been settled within the Empire, and Theodoric their leader had spent his youth at Constantinople. The legal code (*Edict*), which recent studies show cannot be attributed to Theodoric personally but certainly refers to Ostrogothic Italy, is a mere summary of Roman law, principally criminal law, meant to apply equally to Goths and Romans. Nor did the fresh allotment of one-third of all land to the Gothic newcomers make much perceptible difference to the economic state of the country. The Goths were stationed mostly in the north and east of the peninsula, while the south and Sicily were simply garrisoned by small detachments; and for land they could draw on the vacant holdings of Odoacer's troops or other properties which had long lain unoccupied. As regards government, it is generally agreed that Theodoric attempted no change in the institutions which since Diocletian had controlled the social and economic life of Italy.

All this makes it rather hard to accept what contemporaries wrote in praise of Theodoric's reign as a time of marked economic recovery. It is certainly possible that thirty years of peace from invasion and devastation, of order and relative security, were enough to permit some modest revival in production, trade, and civic life generally. We are in fact told, though with obvious exaggeration, that Theodoric for example ordered the construction of a thousand ships, or again that corn was exported from the ports of Campania and the upper Adriatic to relieve a severe food shortage in Liguria and Provence. We also learn from the annals of the first Gothic War that Naples was an active centre of trade and the residence of many merchants from the east, especially Jews, who urged the population to resistance during the siege with assurances that they could keep the town supplied with provisions. Some account must also be taken of the building done by the Goths, of the royal palaces erected at Ravenna, Pavia, and Verona, and the restoration of the theatre at Pompeii, of the monuments and the walls of Rome, and those of other towns. Similar in purpose was the encouragement given to private individuals who undertook to drain the Pontine Marshes and the swamps round Ravenna, in return for a grant of the land they reclaimed for cultivation. But the favourable impression created by these scattered details is altogether cancelled by the far more authoritative evidence of Theodoric's own Edict, which in its selection of imperial laws, and its occasional tendency to increase their severity, proves beyond a doubt that all the distempers of economic life in fourth-century Italy were as vigorous as ever: the man-power shortage on the land, the insecurity of property, and the violent overbearing of the small proprietors and labourers by the great.

2. THE ITALIAN ECONOMY DURING THE GOTHIC WARS AND THE FIRST YEARS OF BYZANTINE RULE

It would seem, however, that a revolutionary change in the relations between the great landowners and their dependent cultivators was at any rate meditated, from motives of political calculation, by king Totila at the crisis of the Gothic War. What he proposed was to break the strength of the landlords, lay and ecclesiastical, who all sided with the Empire, and win the support of the peasantry by abolishing all their rents and services and simply levying what they owed to the state in taxation. This measure, which would certainly have overturned the existing structure of rural society, was brought to nothing by the Byzantine victory; and with the Pragmatic Sanction of 554, which extended to Italy the laws of Justinian, the Romans (or in other words the wealthy landlords) were reinstated in all the properties and rights they had possessed before the days of the "unspeakable" Totila.

The twenty years of savage war between Goths and Greeks were disastrous for Italy. No doubt the Byzantine chronicler Procopius exaggerated seriously when he counted the number of dead in millions, but his dismal story of reprisals and pillage, dearth and disease, is too precise to be doubted. In the course of the war many cities were twice or several times besieged.

Milan was razed to the ground. Rome and Naples were both sacked and left almost empty of inhabitants. Other towns, to stave off famine, had to send away the people who could neither fight nor work. Yet conditions in the countryside can hardly have been better, if at the end of the war, as pope Pelagius complained, land lay idle for want of cultivators. All that was needed after this, to complete the ruin of Italy, was a prompt and reckless application of the Byzantine fiscal system, which even the prosperous eastern parts of the Empire found it hard to bear. In fact the only acknowledgement Justinian's government made of the abnormal state of the country was to allow a five years' moratorium for all debts contracted in the war, and even this concession was limited to private transactions alone; people behind with their taxes were excused one year's payment and no more. The crushing weight of direct taxation, which continued to bear most heavily on landed property, finally destroyed the class of smaller owners and favoured once again the concentration of estates in very few hands. While the poorer taxpayers preferred to quit their land, or surrender it to become tenants of some local magnate, the greater landowners, who often dominated an entire fiscal district, were in a position to avoid paying the charges due from land vacated by fugitive neighbours. They could also exploit their power to elect the civil governors of the province to obtain privileged treatment. As for the artisan and merchant classes, they still appear, together with their guilds, in certain towns; but only Ravenna, and for a time also Naples, seem to have possessed a true trading community engaged in regular traffic with the east.

3. THE LOMBARD INVASION

Only fifteen years after the Gothic War had reestablished imperial authority all over Italy, the country was afflicted by a fresh invasion, the worst that it had suffered since the time of Attila. In 568 the entire Lombard nation, men and women, young and old, numbering in all barely 200,000 people, were driven by the threat of Mongol attack to leave their home in Pannonia, into which they had moved not long before from northern Germany. They crossed the Julian Alps into Italy and soon overran Venetia and the valley of the Po as far west as Milan. They advanced unopposed along the open highways, avoiding the fortified towns where the Byzantine garrisons had taken refuge. The only place they troubled to besiege was Pavia, possibly because of its important position; it fell at the end of three years, to become henceforward the capital of the Lombard kingdom. Very different was the fate of the defenceless and unwalled towns—luckily not numerous—which blocked the path of the invaders. For the most part they were destroyed, and with such efficiency that some of them, especially in eastern Venetia, which had once flourished under the Empire (like Altino, Aquileia, Concordia), left nothing but their name behind, while others only revived a long time after, often on a new site.

Unlike the Goths, the Lombards had been influenced hardly at all by Roman civilization. Their first published code of laws, the Edict of king Rothari, compiled nearly a century after their settlement in Italy, is written in execrable Latin, replete throughout with barbaric terms. They were as little familiar with the law as with the language of Rome. They entered Italy as enemies, not allies of the Empire, and such they remained for over a hundred years. Apart from war, which often consisted of mere raids for booty, their principal activity was hunting and the breeding of swine and other animals most easily adapted to forest life. The basis of their organization, military, political, and social, was in every case the kindred group (or *fara*), combining several families related by blood, which settled down side by side in the same place, usually in the open country. In this way the Roman towns can have had little attraction for them; only the larger detachments sought the cities, from which in many cases they took their name, and which became the residence of their military leaders (the dukes), and later of the officials (*gastaldi*) appointed to administer the royal demesne.

The primitive nature of the early Lombard state was plainly revealed when the need of a united leadership temporarily passed after the death in violent circumstances of the first two rulers, Alboin and Cleph. The kingdom instantly dissolved into a number of autonomous duchies, which by independent action carried the Lombard conquest several stages further, advancing beyond the Apennines into Tuscany and thence through Umbria and the Abruzzi as far south as Benevento and Lucania.

Nor was perfect unity reestablished when the military menace of Greeks and Franks compelled the dukes to revive the monarchy, after ten kingless years, and solidly endow it by restoring half of the lands they had taken into their possession. Even now the two great duchies of Spoleto and Benevento remained virtually separate principalities and barely acknowledged their dependence on Pavia.

4. THE PARTITION OF ITALY BETWEEN GREEKS AND LOMBARDS

The relations of Greeks and Lombards never became friendly, but thirty years after the invasion they did begin to improve. One reason for the change was the weakness, especially the military weakness, of the Byzantine Empire following the death of Justinian. Another was the gradual conversion of the Lombards to Catholicism, which during the reign of Agilulf and his successors reduced at least one cause of conflict between the two peoples. A true peace perhaps was not reached at any time, but short periods of war were interrupted by increasingly long periods of truce, of which the first, of only three years' duration, was arranged at the instance of pope Gregory I in 598, while the last, beginning in the reign of Rothari, persisted for nearly a century, until the Lombard offensive recommenced in the time of Liutprand. The result was that, about the middle of the seventh century, Italy came to be divided into two parts. By that time the Lombards had conquered all the interior from the Po valley southward, with the exception of Lazio; but their frontiers only reached the sea, on the Tyrrhenian side, in Liguria and Tuscany, and on the Adriatic side from Monte Conero down to the Ofanto and along a short stretch between the mouth of the Po and the Exarchate of Ravenna. In other words, Lombard Italy was at least four times larger than Byzantine Italy, but in economic terms the relationship was practically reversed, since the Greeks retained nearly all the coastal districts. More particularly they held the Adriatic seaboard from Grado to the Po estuary, together with Romagna (the Exarchate) and the Marches to a point below Monte Conero; all Apulia was theirs south of the Ofanto, as well as the Ionian coastlands, Calabria, the duchies of Amalfi, Naples, Gaeta, and Rome, and the islands of the Tyrrhenian sea. While the Lombards therefore were practically cut off from all maritime activity and even neglected to use their two ports of Genoa and Pisa, which seem to have languished for more than three centuries, the ports of Byzantine Italy, of Istria and the Adriatic lagoons, of Ravenna, Ancona, Bari, Amalfi, Naples, Gaeta, and Sicily, all maintained perpetual contacts with Constantinople and the eastern Mediterranean, which at that time were economically the most vigorous and enterprising part of the world.

5. THE STATUS OF THE VANQUISHED ROMANS. THE PROPERTY OF THE CHURCH

To what condition the Roman population was reduced in Lombard Italy will never be certainly known; almost the only information we have consists of two famous passages in the history of Paul the Deacon which defy all exact interpretation. After centuries of debate and repeated appeals for enlightenment to the evidence of archeology and coinage, of legislation and the few written records that survive, the following conclusions may be offered as the most plausible. The crown lands of the Roman emperor and the Gothic king, together with the great estates of Roman landowners, who had either fled or been killed, were taken over by the king, the dukes, and their companions. But the humbler classes of society, the peasant cultivators, free or slave, were probably little affected and remained in much the same condition as before. Beside them, it seems, a certain number of independent freeholders managed to survive, whose only obligation was to pay a tribute in kind to the new landlords. Broadly speaking, the labour of tillage was left to the native population whose status remained unchanged, while the Lombards themselves engaged in warfare, hunting, and pastoral farming, for which Italy at that time offered abundant areas of forest, even in the lowlands, and vast tracts of land gone to waste.

One class of landowners, who came to occupy a distinct place in society during these dark centuries, were the clergy, and especially the monks. Ecclesiastical estates, which had started to form in the reign of Constantine, were greatly increased during the Gothic War, when many wealthy members of the aristocracy sought refuge, peace, and protection in the ranks of the Church. Of the numberless properties which passed at that time into the ownership of religious institutions, the first to be managed in a systematic way were those acquired by monastic orders. The man most responsible for this was St. Benedict (480–543), who in his famous *Rule*, compiled about 534 for the abbey of Montecassino, provided a model for the economic practice of all the Benedictine houses subsequently founded throughout Italy and western Europe. To the duty of prayer and meditation St. Benedict added that of work, to which he assigned a principal place in the daily routine of the monks: 5 hours in autumn and winter, $6\frac{1}{2}$ to $8\frac{1}{2}$ hours in spring and summer. Agricultural work held the first place, and this was not confined simply to supervising slaves, tenants, and wage-labourers, but extended also, whenever necessary, to labour on the land by the monks themselves. Besides farming, some time was also to be spent in craft work, producing articles for sale as well as for consumption.

As pious gifts grew and multiplied in number the estates of the Benedictine houses began to assume impressive dimensions. In Italy, no less than in France and Switzerland, Germany, England, and Ireland, many great monastic establishments of this kind are attested after the seventh century. The most conspicuous, after Montecassino itself, were those of Subiaco, Farfa, Bobbio, Nonantola, Santa Giulia di Brescia, Novalesa, Cava dei Tirreni, and San Vincenzo al Volturno. In every one of these the principal monastery and its daughter houses, which were scattered far and wide wherever the community owned land, came to form centres of estate management, directed by the abbot and his fellow monks, some of whom were set in charge of all work performed indoors and in the fields. Like the Roman villa, the early medieval monastery was equipped with granaries, cellars, and other buildings for the storage of demesne produce and the food-rents of peasant holdings. There were also stables and humble workshops where the monks and a small staff of slaves manufactured many of the goods in daily use by the monastery and its dependent population. In this way monastic communities achieved the indispensable minimum of self-sufficiency, without which they could not have survived in an age of feeble government and urban decay.

Not long after the death of St. Benedict, during the turbulent years of the Lombard invasion, the letters of pope Gregory I (590–604) provide a glimpse of administrative methods on another large aggregation of ecclesiastical properties, the estates of the Roman Church. These estates had so expanded by the end of the sixth century as to rival in size and diversity the great imperial domains, from which in part they were descended. The most arduous problem facing Gregory I seems to have been an acute shortage of labour affecting almost all the groups of estates or "patrimonies" (*patrimonia*) into which the papal property was subdivided for convenience of management. The custom was to entrust each of these patrimonies to a steward (*procurator*), while the various estates in his charge were worked in much the same way as imperial estates and granted out to farmers (*conductores*) whose task it was to supervise the labour of the peasant cultivators and collect the owner's share of the harvest. In return for this each farmer was evidently allowed a holding of his own. It does not appear from Gregory's letters that the papal estates were divided into demesne land, exploited by the landlord at his own expense, and tenant land let to dependent peasants or slaves, nor is there any allusion to tenant labour services. Perhaps the labour shortage had reached such dimensions, at least in certain areas such as Sicily, that even this small degree of collaborative farming was impossible. Certainly in Sicily the pope was compelled to disband his demesne herd of horses because a sharp fall in market prices made the cost of keeping slave herdsmen some twelve times greater than the profits of sales from the herd. The unemployed herdsmen were then assigned as labourers to the different estates. What these papal letters show, in brief, is that the system of management in force about the year 600 on great estates in the districts still unconquered by the Lombards, was essentially the one in use on imperial domains, with the difference, however, that land let to leaseholders (by *emphyteusis*) and to free farmers, dependent peasants and slaves, now predominated over land worked by the owner himself with a staff of servile labourers (*familia rustica*).

CHAPTER THREE

From the Partition of Italy to the Carolingian Conquest (seventh and eighth centuries)

I. LOMBARD SOCIETY IN ROTHARI'S "EDICT"

ONCE the first violent period of invasion was over, and the state of continuous warfare ended, everything seemed to promise a return to more settled conditions in Lombard Italy. A unified state had been reestablished, and during the reign of Agilulf the first conversions from Arianism to Catholicism opened the way for better relations between the conquerors and the conquered. But after Agilulf's death power was resumed by the nationalistic Arian party, which discountenanced all departure from the ancient faith and customs of the race. This conservative feeling found its last and most commanding representative in the person of king Rothari, who reopened hostilities with the Greeks and revealed his intention to perpetuate the traditions of his people by publishing in 643 the *Edict* or collection of Lombard laws which goes by his name.

Rothari's *Edict* extends to 383 clauses, more than half of which are devoted to defining the criminal law and providing a scale of charges for the money composition of offences traditionally settled by the feud. Since the rate of composition varied in every case with the blood-price of the injured person, the *Edict* also discloses the whole class structure of Lombard society. Most conspicuous is the strictly military character still maintained by the Lombard people eighty years after the invasion. The political community was composed of free fighting men whose very name (*arimanni*, *exercitales*) defined them

23

as a class of warriors, and the sovereign folk assembly coincided with the levy of the people in arms. First among the free men were the nobles (*adelingi*), sprung from the clans of ancient lineage. From them the general assembly chose the king, dukes, "hundredmen" (*centenarii*), and "tithingmen" (*decani*), who led the various detachments of the host and who also governed the corresponding judicial and administrative districts established after the settlement in Italy.

The main activity of most free Lombards was warfare and hunting; their land they left to be worked by the dependent population. The highest category among the dependants was composed of persons called *aldi* or *liti*, who although free in status had no place in the army and no political rights. They were probably descended from barbarian tribesmen subjugated by the Lombards before the conquest of Italy; that they also included the vanquished Romans is most unlikely. A good idea of the difference in status between the free *aldi* and the several classes of unfree dependents (*servi*) can be had from comparing the money compensation (*wergeld*) which had to be paid for causing their death:

	gold solidi
for killing an	
aldio	60
servus ministerialis probatus et doctus	50
magister porcarius (a slave) *qui sub se discipulos habet duo aut tres aut amplius*	50
dependent *ministerialis*	25
magister caprarius or *pecorarius*	20
bovarius, attached to the *sala*	20
servus massarius (invested with a holding)	20
servus rusticanus qui cum massario est	16
discipulus of a *magister caprarius* or *pecorarius*	16

This list shows that in Lombard Italy also great estates were divided into two parts: the *sala* or *sundrium*, which corresponded roughly to the demesne land (*pars dominica*) of the Roman villa, and the *massaricium*, corresponding to the dependent tenures assigned to peasants (*coloni* or *massari*). In practice, however, there must have been substantial differences, because the *sala* or *sundrium* was mainly composed of woodland, and this explains the prominent position occupied by the chief swineherd (*magister porcarius*), who had two or three assistants under him. The holdings composing the *massaricium* must often have been quite large if tenants could have other slaves working for them. But there is no indication that any labour services were owed for the cultivation of the lord's demesne. The *Edict* contains no reference to the condition of the subject Romans. There can be no doubt that during the years of invasion and interregnum, and again later during Rothari's war with the Greeks, they suffered bitterly, especially the greater landlords and the gentry. Their numbers too must have been seriously reduced by massacre and flight. Yet just because of its violent character the conquest cannot have had a deep or lasting effect upon the native population, particularly the lower classes. The Lombard conquest was no mass migration of land-hungry multitudes driven by force of circumstances to eradicate or subjugate the ancient inhabitants, reducing them to slavery or serfdom. It was an invasion of warrior tribes for whom fighting represented the most profitable, worthy, and absorbing of all occupations, and who at every stage of their advance into Italy lived principally by plunder. Even when they started to settle down, they did so as an army takes possession of enemy territory. They remained organized solely for war, stationing their clans (*fare*) like garrisons outside and often far away from the towns, and making the local population provide for all their needs. To begin with the supply of foodstuffs and billets must have been the only matter on which victors and vanquished had to come to some kind of legal arrangement, and the principle provisionally adopted was probably the ancient one of *hospitalitas*, whereby the few surviving land-owners, and more often no doubt the peasantry, were obliged to set aside one-third of their habitations and their crops. As for the king, dukes, and nobles, we have seen already that land enough to nourish them lay waiting on the great estates of dead and fugitive landlords and the vast domains of the state, where these had not yet been taken over by the Church.

Apart from this it is not at all unlikely that during the first eighty years of Lombard domination the conquered people were left entirely alone by the ruler to settle their private affairs by their own laws and customs. But their public institutions, including those of local government, almost certainly broke down with the destruction of the landowning class, the *posses-*

sores, who had filled municipal offices. At most some minor position may have survived, like that of the *curator* who supervised the urban revenues and markets; in places perhaps the daily needs of the town population kept alive the ancient guilds of certain simple trades.

2. SIGNS OF REVIVAL UNDER THE LAST LOMBARD KINGS. TOWNS AND TRADE IN THE EIGHTH CENTURY

It is enough to compare the laws of Rothari with those of Liutprand, Rachis, and Aistulf, to see that during the intervening eighty years the economic state of Lombard Italy had radically changed for the better; and this impression is confirmed by the public and private documents of the eighth century, which far outnumber those of the 140 years preceding, and also, in more recent times, by the findings of archaeology and numismatics. The laws of Liutprand and Aistulf, which speak of Romans living under Roman law and of merchants (*negotiatores*) serving in the army, also reveal a quite new division of the free population into classes whose military duties are determined no longer by birth but by wealth. One obvious cause of this revival was the long respite from Lombard war and aggression. As peaceful relations developed with Byzantine Italy, the towns and castles and manors of the interior could not remain for ever unaffected by the trade between the eastern Mediterranean and the Greek cities of the Adriatic and southern Italy. The fact that Lombards and Romans lived side by side within the same city walls also made for improvement. But the strongest influence of all in bringing the two peoples together was exercised by the Church, once the Lombards had all become Catholics and episcopal authority in the towns ceased to be divided.

The evidence of some return, however slight, to the habits of an exchange economy, which is contained in the eighth-century laws, is borne out by other sources, documentary and archaeological, which show that the cities were no longer centres simply of civil and ecclesiastical government but also of trade, that money was in more frequent use, and that traffic along the Po between the Adriatic ports and the towns of the

interior was now a regular activity. Although many cities in
Venetia, and a certain number also in Lombardy and Liguria,
had been utterly destroyed or so badly damaged as to make all
recovery impossible for centuries, there were others like Verona
and Pavia, Piacenza and Lucca, which had come through
almost intact or with energy enough to start at once repairing
their walls, and building churches and palaces for the king (at
Pavia), the bishop, and the more important officers of government. Not that the eighth-century towns were at all similar in
aspect or function to the towns of Roman Italy. Usually their
walls enclosed a very narrow space, part of which we often
find was filled not only with gardens and allotments but also
with farmsteads and fields, meadows, pastures, and even tracts
of marsh. Yet in spite of this not all the elements were lacking
for the restoration of the towns to their proper place as centres
of exchange. From the very first years of the invasion we have
seen that the Roman towns, where not destroyed, became the
chosen seats of government of the greater Lombard officials.
More important than this, the towns were also the seat of the
bishops, who during this period were coming to assume increasing public duties. Not only did the bishops, aided by the
monasteries, look after the poor and sick and provide for the
care of pilgrims, but from time to time they also supplanted the
civil authorities in protecting their fellow citizens from enemy
attack, pestilence, and famine. By the initiative of the bishops
as well as of rich private donors, many lodging houses (*xeno-
dochia*) were built in towns along the roads to Rome, and
although these were founded for the use of pilgrims they must
also have served the convenience of a growing number of
merchants.

It is perfectly true that the larger monasteries, and no doubt
all great landlords, were careful to acquire property in different
districts, often far away, to furnish them with those basic necessities which they could not produce at home. Thus the great
ecclesiastical estates of the Po valley all possessed at least one
oliveyard on the northern lakes and also (after the Lombard
conquest of the Exarchate) a saltpan on the Comacchio lagoon;
the cathedral of Lucca and other Tuscan churches obtained
land for the same purpose in the region of Volterra. In this
way, with the help of the carrying services due from certain of

their tenants, these great ecclesiastical landowners may have managed to provide for their essential needs without recourse to any market; and yet we find that the self-same monasteries owned numerous dependent cells (*cellae*) in Pavia, situated by the city walls near the Ticino river or at the junction of the Ticino and the Po, where they treated and stored a part of their produce, not only for the upkeep of their servants in the city but also for sale to the urban population and to merchants descending the Po. Precisely at this time, in fact, during the first years of Liutprand's reign, a royal charter was issued in 715 to the merchants of Comacchio, granting them special privileges in the payment of toll in the various river ports between the mouth of the Po and Piacenza. The charter dealt with the salt trade, but apart from salt, an indispensable commodity which no natural economy can do without, the Comacchio merchants also carried oil and pepper, the latter coming certainly from Constantinople and other Levantine ports. Most likely they brought along as well some cargo of silk and spices. For a long time these oriental wares had been entering Ravenna, which as capital of the Empire and then of the Exarchate had kept up lively relations with Constantinople for over three hundred years. For their journey back to the Adriatic coast, the barges of Comacchio must have loaded up with foodstuffs, especially grain. The people of the lagoon around the Po delta urgently needed grain, while the large estates of the Lombard plain often raised a surplus. It was probably to serve this down-river trade in farm produce that the great monasteries established cells at Pavia; they are also known to have kept their own boats, which freed them in part from dependence on the watermen of Comacchio and, later on, of Venice.

3. ELEMENTS OF A MONEY ECONOMY; TRADE AND TRADES IN LOMBARD ITALY

Another sign of this first feeble revival of an exchange economy is the rapid growth from Liutprand's time onward in the number of mints. Besides the original mints at Pavia and Lucca, from which most surviving coins come, others sprang up at Pisa, Milan, Seprio, Mantua, Piacenza, Verona, and Treviso, and an independent mint was established at Benevento. This multiplication of mints, all of which issued gold coins (*solidi* and *tremisses*) as well as those of smaller denominations, provides clear proof that, although a natural economy may still have prevailed, many towns were now involved to some extent in commerce. At the same time the issue of *solidi* and *tremisses*, however few in number, suggests that money was needed for international trade, or more precisely for the spices and fabrics imported from the east by the merchants of Comacchio.

The commercial activity stimulated by the traffic on the rivers, by intercourse with traders from the ports of Byzantine Italy, and by the rise of urban markets (which now begin to figure in the records), encouraged the formation of a merchant class, the *negotiantes*, who make their first appearance in a famous law of Aistulf of the year 750, as a distinct social order of evident importance. In this law, which defined what arms the king's subjects had to keep in readiness for war, the merchants were divided into three groups: the *maiores* or *potentes*, the *sequentes*, and the *minores*. The *maiores* were treated like landlords owning seven peasant holdings or more, and required to possess a corselet (*lorica*), shield, lance, and horse; the *sequentes* armed themselves more simply with horse, shield, and lance, while the *minores*, who were probably petty local tradesmen belonging to the humblest class of freeborn citizens, were bound to keep only bows and arrows.

Besides the merchants a fair number of town-dwelling artisans are also referred to in eighth-century documents, among them jewellers, painters, coppersmiths, shoemakers, tailors, and soap-makers. These men were almost certainly free in status. They probably lived round the market-places, and seem to have worked on commission from customers. The most celebrated artisans of this period were the *magistri commacini*, who received a whole chapter to themselves in the laws of Liutprand. Whatever the derivation of their name (from the town of Como or from the phrase *cum machina*, which described the scaffolding used in their work) there seems little doubt that they were itinerant builders and masons, who travelled from place to place as required. They were divided into masters (*magistri*) and apprentices (*discipuli*), and their rates of pay were fixed by law. To some scholars the use of these two words, *magistri* and *discipuli*, and the still more significant fact that the soapmakers of Piacenza owed the royal court a yearly rent of 30 lb. of soap (conferred by Liutprand on the church of Piacenza), suggests the possibility that the late Roman guilds may have survived, not only in Byzantine Italy, where artisan corporations are known to have continued at Rome and Ravenna, but in Lombard Italy as well. And this possibility is strengthened by details preserved from a not much later period in the document entitled *Honorantiae civitatis Papiae*. For many generations constitutional historians have been divided on the question of the early medieval guilds, and their rival theories are important here because they seek support in no less contrary conceptions of the economic state of Italy throughout the Lombard, Carolingian, and feudal periods. If artisan guilds did in fact persist in Lombard Italy, whether producing for the market or working to the order of individual customers, then it follows that many Roman cities not only survived the invasions but also continued to function, however inconspicuously, as centres of trade and humble manufacture for the resident population and the neighbouring countryside. According to the opposite view, however, not the towns but the great estates were the centres of all production. These, we are told, were organized on the basis of a strict division of labour: on the one hand were the peasants and herdsmen, living in their scattered farms and huts, on the other the manorial craftsmen, of servile condition (*servi, ministeriales*), gathered into specialized groups under the direction of a master (*magister*). From these dependent groups of slave artisans the free craft guilds were descended, which later came to birth in the time of the city commune.

It may well be that no final answer can ever be given to this controversial problem, which so few documents survive to illustrate. But if the second theory, of seigneurial origins, may be plausibly applied to certain northern countries, where no town life developed in the early Middle Ages, it has little cogency for Italy. Although workshops (*gynaecia*) existed on the great estates of some Italian monasteries, where slave-women spun and wove wool, and although other slave-crafts are attested on Italian manors, the country population of Italy never became entirely independent of the city. This was why urban markets grew and multiplied, and why in the towns, especially those on the main highways and communications, merchants and free artisans continued to thrive, some of whom at least must still have been organized in guilds of the Roman type, if only to manage their relations with the royal exchequer.

4. BYZANTINE ITALY IN THE SEVENTH AND EIGHTH CENTURIES. THE ORIGINS OF VENICE

As far as can be judged, economic conditions were not greatly different in the parts of Italy which remained under Greek domination after the general peace of 680. The form of government is one proof of this. To begin with, a strict separation of civil and military powers had been established by the Pragmatic Sanction of Justinian (554), which extended imperial law to the conquered provinces of Italy; but this system was never given time to work. During the Lombard invasion and the hundred years of almost constant war which followed, the control of government passed once again to the army. As time went on, the army leaders (the exarch and his subordinates, the *magistri militum*, dukes and tribunes) intervened increasingly in civil affairs, until they finally supplanted altogether the prefect and other officials. Except at Naples, which retained some commercial importance, and Ravenna, where the exarch and other great officers resided, municipal government also disappeared after the sixth century, in Byzantine as completely as in Lombard Italy. In the numerous fortified centres or *castella* built by the government for defence, and in the many small towns which sank to the same condition as *castella*, military garrisons commanded by a tribune took the place of the Roman municipality and its ancient corporation of magistrates (*curia*).

The predominance of the army also affected economic life, mainly because, in Italy as in other parts of the Byzantine Empire, the government could never afford to maintain a large permanent body of troops, and therefore had to recruit local militias to defend the frontier castles, which ran the length of the country from Grado to Lucania. Like the Roman military colonies of the past, these garrisons were partly supported by grants of land, which they either worked themselves or put to farm; otherwise the neighbouring peasants and landlords had to keep them supplied. One social effect, no doubt, of the grant of military holdings was to raise the number of small peasant proprietors; but in course of time it also helped to raise the authority of the greater landowners, many of whom managed to get control of both the land and the leadership of their local garrisons and so acquire the power of petty lords.

In spite of obvious similarities, however, there was one important difference between the two Italies: their relation to the sea. Although the Lombards eventually extended their dominions as far as the coasts of Liguria and Tuscany, to part of the gulf of Salerno and along the Adriatic seaboard from Monte Conero to Monte Gargano, there is not the slightest hint in any document that they used these conquests to develop sea-faring enterprise. Even at Genoa no mariners of merchants are recorded before the tenth century. Very different were the conditions in Byzantine Italy. The wide expanse of the Venetian lagoon, which at that time stretched from Grado to the mouth of the Adige, and the network of rivers and canals which inter-sected it, provided safe and easy communication between Istria and the Exarchate. Further south lay the maritime towns of Comacchio and Ravenna and the smaller ports of the Penta-polis. Through them, and even more perhaps through the ports of southern Italy, constant relations were maintained with Sicily, the coasts of the Aegean, and Constantinople, which at that time was the greatest economic centre of the Mediterranean. In cities like Ravenna, Comacchio, and Naples, the pulse of life beat more quickly than in the inland towns of Lombard Italy, at least before the reigns of Liutprand and Aistulf. And the same perhaps was true already of Bari, Amalfi, and Gaeta. To these ports Greek and Syrian merchants brought their fabrics, spices, and oriental wares, and this they continued to do when the Moslem wars of conquest had isolated much of the western Mediterranean from contact with the Levant. By means of these ports even the interior regions of Italy were faintly in-fluenced by the eastern trade, to which Comacchio and the streams of the Po valley opened most of the Lombard plain, and the southern ports gave entry to the Byzantine duchies of Campania and Rome and the Lombard duchy of Benevento.

One part of Byzantine Italy was predestined to particular

importance. This was the Venetian lagoon. The century or more which intervened between the Lombard invasion and the peaceful settlement of the Lombard–Byzantine frontier is the period which historians usually have in mind when they speak of the "origins" of Venice. The long chain of lagoons and islands which separates dry land from sea, and which during antiquity and the early Middle Ages covered the whole coastline of modern Venetia, was certainly not deserted in imperial times; but its only inhabitants then were humble communities of fisherfolk, boatmen, and salt workers. It was the Lombard invasion and subsequent penetration of Venetia which transformed the region by driving the rich and honourable families of the mainland towns to fly for refuge to the islands. Thus Grado, at the far northern end, received the fugitives from Aquileia, and Caorle those from Concordia; the citizens of Oderzo migrated to Heraclea (Cittanova) and Equilio (Iesolo), while those of Altino settled in Torcello and those of Padua and Monselice in Malamocco and Chioggia. Cut off as it was from the mainland by physical geography, political allegiance, and even, for a time, by religious confession as well, the lagoon country continued to form, with Istria, a province of Byzantine Italy. Like all the castles of the Exarchate, the little towns which grew up on the islands were governed by military officers or tribunes, chosen in all probability from the landowners, who had moved from the Roman cities of the hinterland. Not before the end of the seventh century, at the earliest, were the tribunes placed under the command of a duke (*dux*); and the duke was first of all appointed by the imperial government, and only elected locally after the general revolt of Byzantine Italy against the iconoclastic legislation in the eighth century. Even then it would be premature to speak of any breakaway from the eastern Empire; on the contrary Byzantine influences long remained evident in the titles of the Doge (*dux*), the ceremonial of his court and the nature of his power, as well as in the whole orientation of Venetian politics and economy.

The oldest surviving record that touches the economic life of the lagoon people before the Lombard invasion is a famous letter of Theodoric's minister, Cassiodorus, addressed to the "maritime tribunes" (*tribuni maritimorum*) of Venetia. For the

33

purpose of transporting wine and oil from Istria to Ravenna, Cassiodorus enlists the services of the Venetians, who "possess many ships", are "equally at home on sea and land", and who "have the opportunity, when barred from the sea by raging winds, to choose a safer route to travel by way of charming rivers". The writer evidently knew the Venetians' country personally, for he goes on to describe in vivid phrases how "their boats, when partly concealed from a distance, seem to glide across the meadows; and since they are drawn by ropes, the natural order of things is reversed, and men help ships with their feet". Cassiodorus then describes the islands washed on the eastern side by the sea,

"where the tidal ebb and flow alternately covers and uncovers the face of the fields and men have chosen to live like waterfowl, protecting themselves from the onset of the sea by defences of twisted osier. The only wealth of the inhabitants", he explains, "consists in fish; so that rich and poor live on equal terms and the same kind of food and shelter does for everyone. Envy is unknown to them, and their only rivalry finds outlet in the exploitation of their saltworks. Instead of ploughs and sickles they roll their cylinders, and from this source arise all their profits, since all the world has need of salt, and by means of salt the Venetians may possess what they themselves do not produce."

A sharper division of social classes must have followed the first migrations from the mainland, when wealthy landlords, both lay and ecclesiastical, with their company of servants and slaves, invaded the older society of seamen, salt workers, and fishermen. Not that these landlords, whose estates now lay in the territory of a foreign and often hostile power and therefore yielded very uncertain revenues, could hope to emulate the power of proprietors who lived on their own domains. For this reason even the nobility—if any existed—must have tried to balance their failing income from land by taking part, directly or indirectly, in the local forms of enterprise: in the transport of goods by sea and river, in the salt trade, and in the working of the saltpans which existed in great numbers not only at Chioggia but also at Murano and Rialto itself. The sea and river trade in particular must have prospered rapidly after the

Lombard conquest of Ravenna. By the ninth century, and possibly even before, the Venetians had established commercial relations with Sicily, Greece, and Egypt; and from time to time they even penetrated as far as these countries themselves. In the early ninth century we find them possessed of a war-fleet, which they sent to the aid of the Greeks. At the same time we come across them at Cremona and Pavia, as rivals of the merchants of Comacchio, selling not only their salt but also precious skins and feathers, velvets, silks, and Tyrian purple cloth, all of which were oriental products imported in exchange for timber, iron, and above all slaves.

From just this critical period about the year 800 when Venice, with its government now established at Rialto, was first emerging as a maritime power, there have chanced to survive the wills of two Venetian notables, Giustiniano and Orso Partecipazio, who belonged to one of the oldest families and held the offices of Doge and bishop respectively. These documents show quite clearly that the wealth of the Venetian aristocracy had already acquired the composite character it retained until the sixteenth century, and combined in balanced proportions both income from land and the profits of capital invested in loans and trading ventures. Apart from numerous family properties located on the islands and round the lagoon, as well as other estates which they had acquired in the Dogado and territory of Treviso, the Partecipazio had substantial sums invested in overseas trade, which also accounts for the quantity of pepper and other spices disposed of in their will.

It is perfectly evident, therefore, that by the early ninth century Venice was already beginning to profit by its relations with the eastern Empire and its position as intermediary on the frontier between the Byzantine world and Lombard and Frankish Italy.

CHAPTER FOUR

Economic Conditions in Carolingian and Feudal Italy

I. LOMBARD ITALY UNDER THE CAROLINGIANS

THE dispossession of the Lombard dynasty in 774 did not seriously disturb the state of the realm. The Lombard kingdom remained as before, and the title "King of the Franks and Lombards", assumed by Charlemagne after the fall of Pavia, expressed the only manifest change which followed his victory over Desiderius. Two states were now united in the person of a single ruler, but each retained its national laws and institutions, at least in the early years. With a few exceptions like Cividale and Treviso, which had to be reconquered after rebellion, every district continued for nearly thirty years to be governed by dukes and other Lombard officials. Only in 801, after Charlemagne had been crowned Emperor, were the dukes slowly replaced by Frankish counts, and the codes of the Lombard kings supplemented by new Frankish laws (capitularies), some of which were of a general nature while others were particular to Italy.

In order to render their power secure without the effort of planting colonies or garrisons of Franks throughout the country, the Carolingian monarchs made increasing use of the system of "benefices", which now for the first time crossed the Alps into Italy. By this system the confiscated lands of the Lombard king and other Lombard leaders were conferred by means of life grants (which in time were supplanted by full ownership) on the counts and other crown officials, on royal vassals who had settled in Italy, and on a large number of monasteries, many of which now began to accumulate enormous concentrations of property. It seems likely therefore that the Carolingian conquest produced no profound change in the economic structure of the country, and that its principal effect, apart from the substitution of one ruling class of landed magnates for another, was to promote still further the formation of large estates, especially church estates.

It also encouraged the tendency, of some great landlords at least, to seek complete autonomy, administrative, judicial, and economic, and to produce as much as possible on their own domains by exploiting properties in different places which varied in soil and climate. But as we have seen already, the need for economic self-sufficiency was less compelling in Italy than in the Carolingian territories north of the Alps. In Italy the towns had survived and trade was maintained by the ports of the Byzantine provinces with Constantinople and other Near-Eastern cities. It was rather the effect of Charlemagne's policy to make the eastern trade more active than before, and this was sufficient to save Lombard Italy from the fate of the other western countries, which according to Pirenne were condemned to total economic isolation by the Arab conquest of the Balearics, Spain, and Sicily, and the Arab raids on the coasts of Provence, Liguria, and Tuscany. By his account, western Europe in the eighth century was entirely cut off from the far more civilized and economically advanced communities of the eastern Mediterranean, and the last vestiges of Roman culture finally died away.

The difference between Lombard Italy and the rest of the Carolingian Empire is partly revealed by the monetary system. Thus, in the northern countries at this time, gold was no longer coined, but only silver, and this silver currency, based on the *denarius* with a silver content of little more than 2 grams, evidently satisfied the needs of what slight internal trade was carried on in an almost entirely closed and natural economy. In Italy, by contrast, the imperial mints certainly adopted the Carolingian system, but gold coins were still issued in the duchy of Benevento, and the Byzantine *aureus* continued to circulate in all the greater Italian markets, which maintained direct or indirect contacts with the eastern Empire.

But if we are bound to conclude from this and other evidence

that in Italy neither local nor international trade ever ceased
entirely, we must also avoid the opposite extreme of those who
represent the age of Charlemagne as a period of renaissance,
not only in art and letters, but in economic enterprise as well.
That the court of Charlemagne became the centre of a genuine
cultural revival is not in doubt; but in this revival, which was
limited in any case to ecclesiastical circles, Italy played a very
modest part. As for the alleged improvement in social and
economic life, this is hard to prove and difficult to reconcile
with conditions prevailing at the time. For the introduction into
many parts of Italy of the Frankish system of benefices, whereby
the vassals and officials of the Carolingian kings were encouraged
to combine their authority as royal representatives with their
influence as tenants of vast domains, dangerously disrupted the
state and conferred still greater power on the class of landed
magnates, who now began to exercise almost sovereign rights.
They imposed their jurisdiction on their tenants, free and slave,
and increasingly encroached upon the independence of many
humbler landowners, who agreed to accept their protection for
fear of even worse. The effect of this in Italy, as everywhere else,
was not only to postpone for centuries the achievement of
political unity, but also to hinder the growth of a trading
economy with its proper centre in the towns. Indeed, the greatest
obstacle to trade, which only certain areas favoured by their
situation were able partially to overcome, arose precisely from
these small territorial lordships which developed in the country
districts and along many major highways, and tended to restrict
the natural range of urban and market influence.

2. NEW THREATS OF INVASION: ARABS, HUNGARIANS, SLAVS, AND NORMANS

The tendency to political separatism which, despite its oecu-
menical pretensions, underlay the whole Carolingian order,
was powerfully advanced by the wars of succession among
Charlemagne's heirs and their descendants, and even more by
the approach of new and harassing dangers from outside in the
second half of the ninth century. One threat came from the
Arabs, who during the eighth century had occupied the North

African seaboard, Spain, and the Balearics, and early in the ninth century had conquered Sicily and sought a foothold in Sardinia and Corsica. The Arabs generally behaved with tolerance and restraint in their subject territories, which therefore came to enjoy conditions of life far above anything known in the Christian West; but outside their own dominions they remained marauders, and continued for more than a century to visit the coasts of southern France and Italy, not as peaceful neighbours or merchants, but as enemies and pirates bent on plunder and destruction. On the Adriatic side of Italy they took possession of Bari and held it for thirty years; but their favourite haunt was the Tyrrhenian, where they built themselves bases for systematic depredations. One base lay to the south, in the hills above the Gulf of Gaeta, and from here they terrorized Campania and Lazio and threatened Rome itself. Further north detachments of Arabs from Spain installed themselves at Fraxinetum (Garde Frainet), on the seaward slopes of the Provençal Alps, whence for almost a century they plagued the surrounding countryside, selling their captives into slavery. Not only Provence but Piedmont and Liguria also suffered heavy damage from their attacks; the western Alpine passes became too dangerous to cross; and the ports of Genoa and Pisa, threatened by land and sea, were prevented from carrying on any kind of trade.

Towards the end of the century an even worse danger developed, with the advance into Europe of the Hungarians, a central Asian people who overthrew the kingdom of the Moravians and occupied the whole middle Danube plain (the region later known as Hungary). From there they spread in all directions. In 899 they made their first raid into Friuli and the Veneto, laying waste the country as far as Padua. Laden with booty they made their way home in the following year, and then for a time turned their attention to Germany; but Germany was too poor a land to satisfy their appetite for plunder, and so in wave after wave they took the road for Italy again. In 921 they appeared before Brescia; in February 922 they reached Apulia; then in 924 they returned to the Veneto and Lombardy, spreading devastation like the wind. They took the capital, Pavia, where according to the chronicler they destroyed no

fewer than forty-four churches; from Lombardy they passed into
Piedmont, crossed the Alps, and then ravaged the whole of
southern France with fire and sword. Nor was this the end.
For many years they continued their raids, sometimes traversing
the whole peninsula, as in 947, when they pushed down as far
as Otranto.

The Hungarians finally ceased their attacks about the middle
of the tenth century, as they settled down peacefully and permanently on the Hungarian plain. Meantime, certain Slav
tribes had started to move westwards and southwards, descending from Carniola into Friuli, where some of them made their
home in the country south of the Julian Alps and further off to
the west towards the Tagliamento and Livenza. A few of these
colonies have persisted to the present day in the upper Natisone
valley; of the rest the only record now survives in place-names.
Other groups of Slavs advanced from the Balkan peninsula and
planted themselves on the Adriatic coast, which they later made
unsafe for shipping by acts of piracy.

The last intruders of all were the Normans, descendants of the
intrepid seafaring peoples of Scandinavia, who had been a
serious menace under the last Carolingian kings, and finally
obtained, as the price of peace, a grant of the large stretch of
territory on the English Channel which still bears their name.
At the end of the tenth century they made their appearance in
the Mediterranean, not however as invaders, but as soldiers of
fortune, who by deft intervention in the wars between Bene-
ventan Lombards and Greeks, and then between Greeks and
Arabs, eventually won for themselves political dominion in
Apulia and Sicily.

3. THE FEUDAL SYSTEM

The renewal of foreign invasion and the incessant attacks from
outside, which brought widespread disorder to the recently
revived Empire of the West, also ensured the long threatened
triumph of feudalism in almost every country forming part of
the Empire. This was the result of two different movements, one
from below, the other from above. The first of these was of a
kind common to all periods and places in which the state is too

feeble to guarantee justice and security to its subjects. In such circumstances, as we have seen already during the military anarchy of the third century, and again later during the worst times of barbarian invasion, a notable number of small and middle-class landowners, who felt themselves abandoned by the state to the violence of barbarians and outlaws, to the abuses of officials and the encroachments of neighbouring magnates, were forced to turn for protection to some member of this same magnate class, and submit themselves to him by a formal act of commendation (*commendatio*), which reduced them from free proprietors to the condition of tenants bound by ties of dependence to a lord (*dominus*). In legal terms commendation was a purely private contract, but its practical effect was to increase more and more the property and power of the greater landowners, particularly the ecclesiastical landowners, who now became true "lords" of their estates and began to exercise, in fact if not as yet in law, extensive public rights, not only over their own dependent cultivators but also over the numerous class of free *accomendati*.

The movement from above was also caused by the weakness of the monarchy, and more particularly by the king's dependence on patrimonial forms of income. It began in Frankish Gaul during the last years of the Merovingian dynasty and reached its peak under Charlemagne's successors. The only means the king possessed of rewarding and securing the service, especially the military service, of his followers, was to grant them land in benefice or fee in return for an oath of fealty and an act of homage, which made them his vassals and "men" (*homines*). Fief and fealty were the two fundamental and complementary elements of the feudal system which now pervaded society. It grew by the process known as subinfeudation, whereby the tenants of the Crown or tenants-in-chief ("in capite", whence their name *capitanei*, or *cattani*, in Lombardy) conceded part of the land the king had granted them to their own personal vassals, either temporarily or for life. In this way a chain of tenure was created which descended from the king to the humblest class of vassals. At first fiefs held directly of the Crown were granted on revocable temporary terms, generally for life, but in 877, by the capitulary of Kiersy, the monarch was forced to declare them hereditary. By this act the greater feudatories were transformed into almost sovereign independent lords. At the same time they managed to withhold any similar concession from their own vassals down to the early eleventh century, and so retained a powerful means of controlling their tenants, which the rulers had lost. Feudalism therefore became a form of political and social organization, the form assumed by a state in dissolution. All that the king could count on now was the revenue and man-power of his own estates; in everything else—finance, war and foreign policy—his freedom of action was curbed and often cancelled by the need to seek consent from the feudal magnates. Royal authority was compromised still further by the conversion of the greater offices of provincial government (those of count, viscount, and margrave) into hereditary fiefs, and even more by the grant of "immunities", which became especially frequent after the second half of the ninth century. These grants, as their name implies, were originally negative in character and simply declared the beneficiary "immune" from the payment of specified taxes and services and from interference by public officials in certain judicial actions. Later on, however, they began to convey positive rights and permit the immunist himself to receive the taxes and services and exercise some power of jurisdiction over the dependent population of his fief.

4. THE ECONOMIC NATURE OF FEUDALISM

In society and government the feudal system, which prevailed in Lombard Italy from the time of the last Carolingian kings down to the final triumph of the city commune at the end of the twelfth century, possessed an obvious character of its own, representing as it did the total breakdown of the state and the irresistible predominance of local over central power. But economically it differed hardly at all from the system prevailing earlier. What is often called economic feudalism was in fact nothing more than the economic system evolved by the owners of great estates during the late Roman Empire and the barbarian invasions. It is true that certain practices such as commendation and enfeoffment, which helped to develop feudalism, also helped to enlarge and often to combine great estates in the hands of a relatively small number of lay and ecclesiastical lords; but the methods of estate management were not in the least affected. However much involved in the feudal system secular lords, churches, and monasteries might become, the only properties over which they exercised effective economic control were their own estates, and these were divided as before into tenant land and demesne land. The demesne land, much of which was simply pasture and wood, was cultivated partly by the labour of manorial slaves, but mainly by that of free and servile tenants, who owed the lord services as well as small quantities of food and money rent. Labour dues varied with peasant status and the size of holdings, and ranged from a number fixed wholly at the lord's discretion to a regular three or four days each week or a mere handful of boonworks at harvest-time.

The typical fief was formed of several parts. Usually it included one or more fortified centres or castles, built in most cases by the lord himself, but sometimes by groups of small proprietors for their own defence. There were also villages and hamlets, which often gathered together side by side the dependent cultivators of different landlords, and round the villages were scattered homesteads in the open country. Last of all were the manors (*curtes*) or parts of manors, some of them allodial, some held in fee of the Crown or a feudal magnate, some acquired by commendation from lesser landowners seeking protection. Thus a feudal lordship was in no sense an economic unit, but a combination of units, economically subservient to the castle, the manor, the village, or the town, according to their situation.

Bishops, abbots, and secular lords, even when invested with feudal rights, still confined their economic activity to the manors on their own estates, and these as we have seen were still divided into tenant and demesne land. Throughout the ninth and most of the tenth century, the peasant holdings continued to provide most of the labour on the demesne. The few remaining slave labourers may have sufficed for managing the wood and pasture land, but without the services, in most cases heavy, which were exacted by custom or contract from dependent tenants, no arable farming would have been possible at all. We may conclude from this that agricultural production was the

primary purpose of what is called the "manorial" or "seigneurial" system, a system which occupied some thousand years
of European history and reached its maximum development
between the ninth and the eleventh centuries. It is certainly
wrong, as we have said already, to speak of a manorial economy,
and even more a feudal economy, as a comprehensive economic
system, and to suppose that industry and trade, like agriculture,
were confined within the boundaries of great self-supporting
estates, which no goods ever entered or left and which had no
use for money. Admittedly, we find in the records of many
wealthy monasteries, as well as some bishoprics of the ninth
and tenth centuries, definite proof that trades of a kind were
practised at the lord's manor and even in the cottages of
tenants. Thus the famous Brescian monastery of S. Giulia,
which possessed enormous estates divided into 60 different
manors, served by over 700 slaves and 800 tenant families,
employed some of its slaves of both sexes in the production of
homespun cloth, agricultural implements, and unworked iron.
Again the monastery of Nonantola sent twelve *conversae* every
year to the dependent house of S. Michele Arcangelo in
Florence, to sew wool and linen shirts. But beside this evidence
must be set the fact that the labour dues of tenants included
carrying services from one manor to another, often over long
distances, and possibly also from inland manors to the ports
of the Po and its tributaries. At Pavia, as we have seen, the
greater monasteries of the Lombard plain all maintained cells,
built for the most part along the city walls beside the Ticino.
This suggests that some large monasteries at least were in the
habit of selling surplus produce not needed by the monks or the
tenant population. It also affects the question of market rights,
which were granted with great frequency by royal and imperial
privilege during the tenth and eleventh centuries. Some
historians have argued that these rights were different in purpose when granted to great landowners and when granted to
bishops, who were representatives of their towns. Markets of
the first kind, misleadingly called "manorial", they regard as
centres of exchange within the lord's estates, and so as just
another proof that great estates were economically closed;
"episcopal" or urban markets, on the other hand, were intended
from the start for trade with the outside world. But given the

purely fiscal character of market rights and the fact that all movements of produce within manors and between manors was taken care of by the customary and contractual duties laid on tenants and by other administrative arrangements, it is hard to see why lords should have needed markets for the purpose or the revenue from markets, which normally belonged to the Crown. The truth must surely be that markets granted to landowners were also meant for trade with the world outside.

There were only two features of the feudal system which may have had some indirect influence on economic life: the *castellum* and the immunity. The building of *castella*, or fortified villages, had been going on for centuries; but it was during the feudal age that castles began to spring up everywhere in response to the threat of foreign invasion and internal disorder. Some were erected by feudal lords, some by the people of the countryside, who moved to the castle for protection; but whatever their origin, they all ended up, in fact and frequently in law, under the control of a *dominus*, who built himself a stronghold there (*belfredum*) for defence and domination or as a convenient place for storing produce from his subject lands. In this way the castle not only replaced the manor, but often became a centre of defence and government, justice and economic life; and its authority extended not only over the lord's own dependants, but also over many free peasants and small proprietors, who settled with their huts and households inside the castle walls.

The grant of immunities did even more to enhance the power of feudal lords, lay and ecclesiastical. For an immunity conferred military, judicial, and fiscal rights over the entire territory held in fee, and so entitled the lord to exact by public authority charges and services additional to those already due by private contract or custom from his tenants. When lords acquired the right to levy tolls and demand services for the construction, maintenance, and guard of castles, for river regulation and other public works, when they assumed jurisdiction in minor cases, and most of all when theirs became the only power in a district, unchecked even by the king, then inevitably economic life in all its phases was affected. In particular the progress of feudal lordship threatened to reduce all classes of the peasant population to a uniform condition of dependence. This is why, from the tenth century on, we find

45

increasing evidence of protests, lawsuits, and outright revolts directed against feudal abuses, arbritary impositions and *superimpositiones*, which the peasantry refused to recognize as either warranted or just.

CHAPTER FIVE

Beginnings of Revival in
the Tenth and Eleventh Centuries

I. THE CITIES OF BYZANTINE ITALY:
RAVENNA, ROME, BARI, AMALFI

AMONG the causes of change in the social and economic order of the countryside, some of which as we shall see were purely internal, was the steady growth of trading connexions with the East by way of Byzantine Italy. Both the provinces which were still occupied by the Greeks and those which had passed since the time of Pepin under the nominal if ineffective rule of the papacy had certainly suffered the same desolation and depopulation as the rest of Italy; but society had not yet surrendered to the feudal system, at least in the south and islands, where feudal institutions were only introduced by the Normans in the eleventh century, and in Sardinia by the Aragonese in the fourteenth.

It was not so much the forms of rural organization, however, which differentiated the papal and Byzantine regions from other parts of Italy, as the precocious development of the towns, especially those near the coasts. Ravenna, it is true, had declined since the days when it served as the capital of the western Empire, and then of Gothic and Byzantine Italy. The brief but calamitous Lombard occupation under Liutprand was followed almost immediately by annexation to the Papal States, which detached the city from Byzantium and deprived it of its status as a capital. Even so Ravenna preserved something of its prosperous past. It was still the seat of one of the richest and most powerful bishops in Italy, and was still the home of numerous *negotiatores* and of various categories of artisans, some

47

of whom the records show to have been organized in guilds (*scholae*).

Rome, during the barbarian and feudal age, was the merest relic of the great metropolis that had once ruled the Empire in its prime. The population, which had reached at least a million between the age of Augustus and that of Trajan, seems to have fallen by the end of the sixth century to a bare 30,000 or 40,000 souls. Yet even at this desolate time the city retained a certain importance, partly as the seat of the Roman duchy, but far more as the centre of the Catholic Church, to which men were drawn from all over Europe. Not only did great prelates journey there with their retinues, but also large numbers of pilgrims of all classes and countries, from the British Isles and Scandinavia, the Low Countries, Germany, and France. At Rome the Anglo-Saxons, the Frisians, the Franks, the Lombards, and the Hungarians all possessed national churches with their own lodging-houses and burial-grounds. In the wake of these foreign visitors, who brought rich gifts to the city and set in motion a considerable circulation of money, came also foreign merchants; and beside the foreign merchants existed native merchants and many artisans, skilled in specialized trades and organized, like those of Ravenna, in guilds (*scholae*) with their own officials. But what especially distinguished Rome from all other western cities at this time was the presence of professional money-changers (*cambiatores*), who dealt in the various currencies brought from abroad, and were probably already advancing loans to local churches and the papal court itself.

Far more important economically than either Rome or Ravenna were the seacoast towns, which after the Arab expansion in the western Mediterranean remained the sole intermediaries of such trade as survived between East and West. One such town was Bari on the Adriatic coast, which for a long time had been the object of conflict between the Greeks and the Lombards of Benevento and had then fallen into Arab hands (840–70). It was finally recovered by the Byzantines, who made it their capital in southern Italy for more than a century. As a result Bari was brought into close connexion with Constantinople, for purposes not only of government but also of trade. In the chronicles we read of pilgrims embarking at

Bari for the Holy Land, and of ships from Bari laden with the merchandise of Calabria and Durazzo, the Morea and Constantinople. The famous Golden Bull granted by the Emperors Basil and Constantine to the merchants of Venice in 992 forbade them to ship any cargoes on behalf of Amalfitans, Jews, or Lombards of Bari. The object of the prohibition was to prevent other traders from exploiting the reduction of customs duties accorded to the Venetians; but it also shows incidentally that about this date the citizens of Bari and Amalfi were regular customers in the great market beside the Bosphorus. During the same period the merchant ships of Bari were visiting ports in Syria and Asia Minor, and it was ships plying these routes which seized the relics of St. Nicholas at Myra in 1087. The great church of St. Nicholas, built to house them, and the magnificent cathedral of Bari both testify to the wealth of the city in the eleventh century.

Even more active was the trade developed at this time by the southern ports of the Tyrrhenian. The three Byzantine duchies of Amalfi, Naples, and Gaeta, which were cut off from the other Greek dominions of southern Italy by the Lombard principalities of Salerno and Capua, were in much the same position politically as Comacchio and Ravenna had been before their subjugation by Liutprand, and as Venice still continued to be. Nominally subject to Constantinople but in practice independent, they were careful to maintain the formal relation of alliance and allegiance with the Empire, for the commercial advantages it offered. But unlike Venice they had other neighbours to contend with, who were more dangerous and more powerful—the Arabs, who from their conquered territory in Sicily and their base above Gaeta not only threatened shipping but also conducted frequent and devastating raids to places far inland. With neighbours such as these the three Greek cities of the Campanian seaboard were quick to seek some kind of peaceful understanding; and it was probably their opportunist policies which decided Byzantium to reserve its special favour for the faithful citizens of Venice. The only city of the three which has left behind much evidence of its former commercial greatness is Amalfi, which undoubtedly held first place among the Tyrrhenian ports from the tenth to the twelfth century. Amalfi, Atrani, and Ravello form three tiny harbours, not more than a few hundred yards apart, on the northern side of the gulf of Salerno, below the precipitous slopes of the Sorrentine mountains. Their astonishing rise to fortune was the product of trade with the Arabs and Greeks and with the Lombards of the hinterland, who as yet commanded no shipping of their own to satisfy the growing demand for the exports of the eastern countries and countries of Mediterranean climate. In the eleventh century the Amalfitans possessed a colony at Constantinople complete with churches and monasteries; they occupied a street in Antioch; and they were frequent visitors to the ports of Egypt, Tunisia, and Spain. In the principal cities of Sicily, during the twelfth century, we find that Amalfitan merchants had their own commercial quarters, all of which dated from the time of Arab rule. The Amalfitans also penetrated into the Adriatic, despite the growing predominance of Venice; they had a colony at Durazzo, and carried merchandise from Sicily to Ravenna. But their main activity at all times lay along the coast of the Tyrrhenian. Rome was one of the markets they frequented most, providing the city and especially its churches with the costly products of Greek and Arab industry and art. Further north they established close relations with Pisa, where they owned shops, with Genoa, and also perhaps with the cities of Provence. In the early eleventh century we meet them in the heart of the northern plain, attending the annual fair at Pavia alongside traders from Salerno, Gaeta, and Venice. At the same time merchants of Arab, African, and Italian nationality dealt together in the streets of Amalfi itself, which the chroniclers describe as a prosperous city, rich in gold, silver, and precious fabrics, and drawing customers from all the country round to come and buy its oriental wares.

From the thriving and multifarious trade of Amalfi certain local families eventually acquired conspicuous wealth and power. The greatest of these were the Pantaleoni, one of whom, Mauro, played a leading part in the politics of eleventh-century Europe and is remembered for his generous gifts to churches, not only in his native town, but also at Rome (S. Paolo fuori le Mura), in Apulia (S. Michele on Monte Gargano), and at Antioch and Jerusalem. But the commercial prosperity of Amalfi was precariously based on the political independence of the duchy, which was never free from threat

by the princes of Salerno and was finally overrun by the
Normans. The blow was mortal. Absorbed into a united kingdom of southern Italy, and deprived almost completely of
autonomous rights, Amalfi, which possessed no natural hinterland, soon found itself outstripped by other ports better
favoured in their situation. Once its primacy had gone it rapidly
declined.

2. THE RISE OF VENETIAN SEAPOWER BETWEEN THE NINTH AND ELEVENTH CENTURIES

With Ravenna in decay and Comacchio in ruins, the only
notable maritime power north of Bari was Venice, though a
number of minor Apulian ports like Trani, Barletta, and
Siponto (Manfredonia) attained to some importance during
these centuries by the exports of corn. The commercial strength
of Venice was more securely based than that of either Bari or
Amalfi, and already in the tenth century Venice outdistanced
both these towns in the trade of the eastern Mediterranean.
Ever since the last years of Charlemagne's reign the Venetian
government (now established at Rialto) had drawn advantage
from the agreements reached between the western and eastern
Empire, touching conditions in the Adriatic. A few years later,
in 840, the so-called *pactum* of the emperor Lothair, which
defined relations between the small communities of the
Venetian lagoon and their neighbours on the mainland and the
upper Adriatic, gave Venice undisputed control over all the
rivers issuing from the Po valley, which was the first and
indispensable condition of commercial expansion in Adriatic
and eastern waters. Apart from certain "good neighbour"
clauses providing for the mutual defence of their subjects and
the pursuit of fugitive slaves, this "compact" of 840 bound the
two contracting parties to observe freedom of trade along the
rivers entering the Adriatic and to levy duty (*ripaticum*) at the
low rate of $2\frac{1}{2}$ per cent by weight or value. In practice this
clause, although reciprocal, worked wholly to the profit of
Venice. The Venetians also engaged to seize no prisoners and
buy no Christians for sale into slavery. While keeping on good
terms with the western Empire, the citizens of the Venetian

duchy maintained their traditional relations of alliance and fealty with the eastern Empire, sometimes to the point of active military collaboration. In return they were rewarded with ample privileges, such as the Golden Bull of 992 already mentioned, which assured them a decided superiority over their competitors from southern Italy. At the same time the Venetians consolidated their position in the upper Adriatic, extending their influence along the western coast from the Po as far as Ancona, and then in the late tenth century across into northern Dalmatia. Though their progress was contested and incomplete, the doge Pietro Orseolo II was none the less pleased to assume the title of *dux Dalmaticorum*.

The intensity of Venetian trade with Byzantium in these years can be inferred from the decree of the doge Pietro Candiano in 960, which forbade Venetians to carry to Constantinople any but public letters and despatches from such regions as Lombardy, Bavaria, Saxony and other parts of Germany. This suggests that Venice was already the port of embarkation and arrival for merchants and pilgrims travelling between the Po valley, Germany, and the Levant. In the following century the Venetians steadily increased their influence in the Byzantine world, until in 1082, on the eve of the First Crusade, they finally attained complete supremacy over their commercial rivals by the privilege of Alexis I, which granted them unlimited freedom of trade throughout the Empire, with absolute immunity from all customs duties and the right to possess shops, warehouses, and landing stages of their own at Constantinople. This last concession, however, did little more than recognize existing conditions; already thousands of Venetians were settled in Constantinople, which served them as a base for trading expeditions to Greece, Macedonia, Thrace, Asia Minor, Syria, and Egypt.

One effect of the flourishing traffic with the East was to stimulate Venetian trade with the hinterland along the river Po. We hear most about this at Pavia, where Venetian merchants in the tenth century brought salt, spices, and luxury articles of dress and ornament, and were permitted on payment of an annual tribute to acquire grain, wine, and certain other agricultural products for export. The evidence contained in the famous Pavian document, the *Honorantiae civitatis Papiae*, which although compiled in the first decades of the eleventh century is clearly inspired by earlier conditions, is fully confirmed by private commercial deeds of the same period. Together they show that the Po trade was nourished less by Venetian salt production than by the seaborne traffic with the Levant and the imports, modest though they were, of oriental spices and perfumes, dyestuffs, silks, and cottons, as well as Greek oil and wine. What western countries had to offer the Venetians in return was poor in comparison, and consisted mostly of timber, a little silver, iron, and copper, and a large number of slaves, especially slaves from Slavonia, whom Venice persisted in shipping to the East, despite repeated prohibitions in treaties of the ninth and tenth centuries.

It would be wrong to speak as yet of commerce on the grand scale, based on massive capital investment and rewarded with large private fortunes. This came later, after the Crusades. But the main features of Venetian trade in its golden age were already apparent in the year 1000.

3. PISA AND GENOA IN THE TENTH AND ELEVENTH CENTURIES

Meanwhile, on the opposite side of Italy, two seafaring communities were growing up, destined after the First Crusade to become the main rivals of Venice in Mediterranean commerce: Pisa and Genoa. The natural development of both had been held back for centuries by political misfortune. First, they had been conquered by the Lombards, a circumstance which cut them off from the only international maritime trade of the time, the trade with the East. Then later, throughout the eighth and ninth centuries, they had been subject to attack and devastation by the Arabs, who as masters of the western Mediterranean had made any commercial revival impossible.

Pisa was a river-port, with a dependent port on the sea (Porto Pisano, just north of Leghorn). It had probably suffered less from the Saracens of Fraxinetum than from those of the south, whose attacks ceased towards the end of the ninth century following their defeat by the allied forces of the pope and the dukes of southern Italy. This fact, and the proximity

of Lucca and the highway to Rome (Via Francigena), permitted Pisa to revive before Genoa. Resistance to the Arabs
was itself a stimulus to maritime trade and warfare. In a short
time the Pisans were able to launch a counter-offensive, and
by the eleventh century their fleets had become strong enough
to venture forth, on their own or with Genoese support, as far
as Calabria and Sicily and even beyond, to the Balearics, Spain,
and Africa. There can be no doubt, as Volpe says, that economic
motives were at work behind these preliminary crusades of
Pisans and Genoese in the western Mediterranean; for although
the expeditions used feudal forces and stirred the appetites of a
petty nobility which was largely country-dwelling, they had the
character and purpose of strictly urban enterprises, organized
by private merchants for the defence of their commercial
interest, for plunder, and for the subjugation, economic rather
than political, of countries rich in precious raw materials. The
countries which Pisa and Genoa were most anxious to win from
Arab influence and domination were Sardinia, Corsica, and
the island of Elba. In the contest which followed Pisa outdid
Genoa, and by the early eleventh century had gained control
of Corsica and possibly of Elba also, at least indirectly through
the ecclesiastical jurisdiction of the Pisan bishop. Sardinia
succumbed less quickly; but in the northern part of the island at
least, after the victory of 1016, the Pisans successfully imposed a
sort of protectorate which gave them extensive trading
privileges.

At Genoa, before the second half of the tenth century, there
was little to recall the flourishing city of Roman times. Even the
walls, destroyed by Rothari, were left to lie for centuries in
ruins; while the site, never large, of the former Roman town was
invaded by cultivated plots and fields and by pieces of waste
interspersed with makeshift houses of wood. Because of neglect
or Saracen attacks, the two Roman roads which at one time met
at Genoa had both been abandoned for a different highway
further to the east, the so-called Via Francigena, which crossed
from Piacenza on the Po by way of the Cisa pass to Luni, near
Sarzana, and in this manner avoided entirely the Arab-infested
coast of eastern Liguria. The decay of Genoa is also reflected in
the fact that it never became the seat of any high official of the
realm. The only authorities to reside in or near the town were

the bishops and the viscounts; and it was under their rule that Genoa started to revive with astonishing rapidity towards the middle of the tenth century, just when Arab power was on the wane. The city walls were now rebuilt and the cathedral church established inside their perimeter. About the same period, in 987, feudal forces from Provence overcame the dreaded Arab stronghold at Fraxinetum and finally removed the threat of Muslim attack by land. This enabled Genoa to join Pisa and counter-attack by sea, with the result that in less than thirty years the northern Tyrrhenian was cleared of the Arabs for good.

This rapid rise to naval power encouraged the Pisans and Genoese to open commercial dealings with the maritime communities of the south: Gaeta, Naples, and Amalfi. They also traded with the Arabs, in the frequent periods of truce with the Saracen world, interrupting their regular pirate raids and visiting the ports of Sicily, Spain, and Africa in the peaceful character of merchants. But throughout the course of the eleventh century there is scarcely any sign of commercial relations with the East. Only after the Norman conquest of Sicily, which freed the Straits of Messina, and more particularly after the First Crusade, in which the Pisan and Genoese fleets played a dominant part, were the two cities able to challenge the power of Venice along the Syrian coast and eventually all over the Levant. In the meantime, during the century before the First Crusade, the measure and intensity of Pisan and Genoese trade, restricted though it was to the western Mediterranean, is revealed in the rapid progress of new building, in the growth of a mercantile middle class, in the evolution of a code of maritime custom, and in the lively concourse of visiting merchants who came from all the coastal cities between Barcelona and Salerno, from the inland parts of Lombardy and Tuscany, and from the countries beyond the Alps.

4. THE REVIVAL OF THE INLAND TOWNS

Not only on the coasts of Byzantine and Lombard Italy but also in the interior of the Italian kingdom the greater vigour of urban life continued to distinguish Italy from the northern countries of post-Carolingian Europe where feudalism had obtained a firmer hold. By the later ninth century we already find several causes combining to increase the importance of many inland towns, especially those along the rivers: the development of trade between the coastal cities and the Byzantine and Arab world, which inevitably affected the hinterland; the needs of defence, which compelled townspeople to build or reconstruct the city walls; and the influx of numerous country folk seeking protection. No doubt the towns of the interior preserved little of the Roman past beyond their names; indeed, with few exceptions, they can hardly be considered towns at all, in the economic sense of densely settled communities engaged in every kind of business other than agriculture. As we have seen at Genoa, fields and meadows covered the greater part of many towns, and the landlords who dwelt there—the bishop, the count, and other officials, together with certain feudal vassals great and small—all had food-rents delivered by their tenants in the country. If we remember also that the towns possessed rights of common in the neighbouring woods and meadows, we can only conclude that land and the income from farming and forests, pasture and hunting, remained the principal support of part, and possibly a large part, of the urban population.

At the same time it is obvious that, however unpretentious their life might be, the great office-holders of church and state who resided with their retinues in the city were quite unable to supply all their needs from local sources. This is why whatever glimpses we get of urban life from the casual names, phrases, and professional titles preserved in the few surviving records and inscriptions of the time, always reveal a complex society, consisting not merely of magnates and clergy, peasants and slaves, but of other groups of people as well, who can only be described as precursors of the later bourgeoisie. We have seen that the laws of Aistulf, published in the last years of the Lombard kingdom, already treat the *negotiantes* as a separate class, divided into three grades, of whom the highest were placed on the same level as the middle class of landowners. There is some doubt whether the term *negotiantes* was used, as in Roman times, to denote persons whose main business was moneylending, or was meant to describe professional merchants. But in view of the limited opportunity presented for credit operations in the small depopulated inland towns of that period, it is much more likely that Aistulf's legislation was addressed to genuine merchants, some of whom no doubt were still itinerant traders, while others, and perhaps the greater number, were permanently resident in the city. So much may be inferred from the numerous licenses granted by the Italian kings, and still more by the Ottonian Emperors, to open markets in the towns or beneath their walls, and also from the names of certain taxes such as *buticaticum, curatura,* and *portaticum,* which clearly refer to a periodic or continuous urban trade. Similarly the places appointed for the payment of river tolls (*ripaticum* and *palefictura*), though sometimes located on the borders of some great landed estates, were normally sited near the towns, particularly the towns which lay along the Po and other navigable rivers or along the highways leading from the Alps to Pavia and Rome. It should be added that the development of markets also encouraged the rise of a class of free artisans, most of whom we find mentioned in market towns. There was one industry, it is true, the cloth industry, in which down to the twelfth century artisans of free condition probably found it hard to compete with the slave-run workshops of the great monasteries; but in other industries they were quite independent of any manorial controls, and indeed were placed under the direct protection of the king. Artisans of this type were the workers in the building trades, the soapmakers and the metal workers (especially those engaged in arms manufacture), the jewellers, moneyers, and skinners.

The most detailed evidence of progress in urban industry and trade, apart from scattered hints in documents and inscriptions, is contained in the *Honorantiae civitatis Papiae,* which were a sort of tract or memorial (*Memoratorium*) written to vindicate the fiscal claims of the Crown on merchandise crossing the frontiers and on monopolies granted by the state to certain trades. Particularly valuable, for the proof they provide that international trade was also carried on by land and across the Alps, are the rules mentioned in the *Memoratorium* regarding the customs stations (*clusae*) of the realm. With the sole exception of three stations situated on the eastern frontier, which was moved towards the lowlands during the Ottonian period, the *clusae*

were all located at the foot of the principal Alpine valleys: at
Susa and Bard, Bellinzona and Chiavenna, Bolzano and then
Valorgne (near the *clusa* of Rivoli). They were fixed, that is, in
places which were easily reached from the plain and at the
same time opened the way to central Lombardy and thence
across the Po, at Cremona, Piacenza, or Pavia, to Tuscany and
Rome. All pilgrims and merchants from north and central
Europe passed through the customs. The pilgrims paid no duty
on their personal effects, but like the merchants they had to
pay 10 per cent on all goods brought in for purpose of trade,
such as horses, slaves, and swords, and woollen, linen, and
hempen cloth. The Anglo-Saxons, for the most part pilgrims,
objected to having their baggage inspected by the customs
officials, and eventually, after long dispute, a special agreement
was arranged between the English king and the king of Lombard Italy which freed them from molestation at the customs,
in return for the payment of a lump sum every three years to the
palace at Pavia of 50 pounds of silver and some gifts in kind.

The geographical position of the customs stations explains the
rise to prosperity after the ninth century of certain towns along
the roads which they commanded, in particular Asti and
Vercelli, Milan and Pavia, Verona, Cremona, Piacenza, and
(just beyond the Apennines) Lucca. The last two towns were
especially fortunate in being situated at vital points on the road
from France and the British Isles to Rome. Piacenza stands
where the Via Francesca crossed the river Po, and as early as
the ninth century it was the meeting-place of four annual
markets each lasting eight days; then in 896 a yearly fair was
also instituted, of seventeen days. Lucca lies at the southern end
of the Garfagnana, not far from the Magra valley and Pisa. It
had been a centre of considerable economic and political
importance ever since the later Lombard period. It possessed a
mint and issued coins which circulated all over Italy as far as
Rome, alongside the money of Pavia; it manufactured luxury
cloth; and its merchants were rich and numerous enough to
secure from the Emperor Henry IV complete exemption from
duty (*curatura*) on all their sales and acquisitions in the markets
from Pavia to Rome.

The *Memoratorium* then, in agreement with other records,
clearly shows that the road system retained some importance

for traffic and trade even during the early Middle Ages; but it also leaves us in no doubt that much the most favoured means of inland transport, at least in the valley of the Po, were the waterways. This was so already in the eighth century, when people travelled regularly up the Po from Venice and Comacchio to Pavia and Milan, putting in at Ferrara, Cremona, and Piacenza. Their way was slow and embarrassed by numerous customs duties, for the rivers were considered public property to be exploited as a source of revenue or granted out on feudal terms to royal officials, religious corporations, and private subjects. And so at every step travellers were held up by agents of the Crown or the feudatories, demanding payments in money or part of the cargo. On goods simply passing through these charges were mostly trifling, but they rose substantially whenever boats were brought in and moored for loading and unloading. We learn from documents that the rivers were used by great landlords who kept simple flat-bottomed boats for moving produce from outlying estates to the central manor, or made their tenants ship from nearby markets the few goods they needed from outside. But this was small-scale transport over fairly short distances. Most river traffic was organized by merchants, some of whom travelled anything up to 200 miles or more, with their shiploads of salt and salted fish, slaves, precious fabrics, spices and drugs, medicines, perfumes, ornaments, and other rare and valuable merchandise. In course of time the Venetians were joined by merchants from other riverside towns such as Ferrara, Mantua, Cremona, Piacenza, and Milan. All of them used the rivers, so that the Po and its tributaries rapidly became flourishing highways of commerce, of which the records of Cremona in the tenth and eleventh centuries give especially rich and lively evidence.

However, the most important commercial centre of the Po valley, for at least three centuries, was certainly Pavia, which only started to decline in favour of Milan after the year 1000. Pavia was the seat of government and financial administration. It was also situated at the junction of the Po and the main roads from the Alps and Apennines; and it was the terminus for most ships coming up river. So the city had every right to be considered the economic as well as the political capital of the kingdom. Down to the late eleventh century the coinage of

Pavia prevailed throughout Lombard Italy. At Pavia the richest monasteries and churches of Lombardy and other regions all had houses or hostels or manorial centres, often with a shop or two, which they rented out to merchants, and with the right to make use of the ports on the Ticino and the Po. So notable a centre of exchange was not frequented only by merchants from other towns, Venice, Amalfi, or Gaeta; the *Memoratorium* informs us that Pavia had its own merchants, "men of great worth and wealth" (*magni honorabiles et multum divites*), who were organized in "mysteries" (*ministeria*) or guilds under royal tutelage and had the special privilege of preemption in all the markets they attended by land or water; by this concession they avoided competition from local traders in whatever business they transacted. Beside the merchants, we find the members of many other Pavian trades and professions joined together in guilds under their own masters; such were the moneyers (*monetarii*), who farmed the mint, the fishermen and boatmen, the soapmakers, and the curriers, who were limited to twelve in all with a like number of apprentices. At Pavia therefore, and probably also at Piacenza, the evidence of the *Memoratorium* makes it certain that towards the end of the tenth century there existed a group of professional and trade associations, controlled and taxed by the Crown, which in return invested them with rights of monopoly. It will be noticed that this system closely resembles the Byzantine guild organization, described about this time in the Book of the Prefect.

The *Memoratorium* also contains one mention of Milan, concerning the mint. The Milanese mint was managed on the model of the Pavian mint under four masters, who like their brethren of Pavia were "rich and noble" men and worked to order for the royal treasury, coining "Milanese pennies" (*denarios Mediolanenses*) equal in purity and weight to those of Pavia, and paying the same annual rent to the Crown of 12 pounds of coin. In other records of the tenth century we frequently read of Milanese artisans and merchants, of whom a good number had acquired property and a position of some importance in society.

5. THE BEGINNINGS OF CHANGE IN THE COUNTRYSIDE

The transformation of urban and commercial life was accompanied by parallel changes in agrarian conditions, for which the documentary evidence, though sometimes inconclusive, is far more copious. What this evidence reveals is the steady breakdown during the tenth century of the system evolved for managing great estates. The balance which had been established between demesne and tenant land, and which guaranteed the owner both a labour force and most of the basic income to be drawn from the land he worked himself, was increasingly disturbed. In the records of this period we can watch the progressive and almost complete disappearance of the household slaves (*praebendarii*), who lived at the manor, were maintained by the lord, and worked exclusively for him, as domestic servants, craftsmen, and sometimes—though not often—as labourers in the fields. From the ninth century on fugitive slaves were frequently the subject of complaint and legislation; but the main cause of declining numbers was not so much flight as a return to the ancient practice by which, ever since the later Roman Empire, countless personal slaves had been converted into tenants (*servi casati*) with a hut and plot of land (*casa et substantia*). By this device lords were able to exact a large number of labour services without having to bear intolerable expense. And yet there seems no doubt that the tenth century also witnessed a substantial diminution in the quantity of labour services rendered by tenants, whatever their status or tenure. Even the humblest class of dependent cultivators (who were possibly descendants of the "servus rusticanus qui cum massario est" of Rothari's laws) were no longer forced to work at the lord's discretion: their duties were fixed by custom, and custom was no longer a personal bond, different for each individual, but a system of rules for the whole estate (*consuetudo fundi, consuetudo loci*), destined a century later to assume great importance as the primitive source of village statute. At the same time that the bonds of servitude were relaxed and the status of hutted slaves improved, there are signs that conditions were also becoming better for the class of peasant leaseholders (*libellarii*), whose relations with the lord were regulated by contract. The contracts were normally grants for 29 years, but since they were nearly always renewed they became in practice perpetual. Labour services do not entirely disappear from peasant leases, but where they survive they are few in number and usually limited to harvest time.

The most obvious effect of all these changes, which began in the tenth century and then came to prevail in the two centuries following, was to disrupt the manorial system at its most sensitive point: the lord's demesne. It was the same on both lay and ecclesiastical properties; the high cost and scarcity of slave labour, and still more the practical obstacles to replacing slave labour by the compulsory services of tenants who lived in scattered farms about the estate, made demesne farming increasingly difficult to carry on. The insufficiency of slave labour may seem hard to reconcile with the unambiguous evidence of slave-trading in this and later centuries. But the fact is that the international slave trade was now no longer supported by massive wars of conquest, but only by the petty raids and forays of the Balkan and other tribes of eastern Europe; and so the slave market could only furnish labour enough for domestic service and specialized crafts. In farm work we have no record of slaves being used at this time. As for the decline of labour services, this was certainly the result of profound changes proceeding in the general economic condition of Italy, which inevitably reacted on rural life.

The growing number of licences to open markets on manors or in castles and towns, the new importance assumed by urban markets in particular, the rise of a class of merchants, some of whom, in the Lombard towns especially, became owners of land and persons of social standing—all this could only stimulate demand for the products of the countryside. And in fact, during the ninth and the tenth centuries, it became increasingly the custom for landlords to stipulate, when granting peasant leases (mostly *libelli*), that a part of the holding should be improved by planting vines, olives, or fruit trees, or reclaimed and sown with corn. In a few cases more ambitious works were contemplated, addressed to flood control, the drainage of marsh, or—very occasionally—irrigation. For the present, large tracts of demesne land, even in the lowlands, were still covered with wood and pasture. On tillage land the leading crop was corn, for the most part wheat, but also sorghum, barley, rye, and millet. The yield was low—generally four- to fivefold—but even so provided landlords with a marketable surplus. Next in importance to cereals were vines, which were widely grown in all latitudes. They were usually interplanted with grain or grass, but were also cultivated apart in tiny vineyards. Indeed the principal object of leases for improvement—*ad pastinandum* as they were called in the south—was precisely to increase the amount of land under vines. On the basis of more than a thousand documents relating to south Italy between the ninth century and the year 1025, Lizier arrived at the following ratio between vines and other new plantations:

	vines	the rest
before 950	1	1
950–975	2·5	1
975–1025	3·25	1

Olive cultivation in particular was much less diffused. It is true that olives were grown in all districts from the Alpine foothills to Calabria, but the number of trees was generally small and production very meagre. We also find far fewer olives being planted than vines: seven vines for every olive according to Lizier's calculations. As for fruit trees, they are even less commonly referred to, and there is no mention at all, on the mainland at least, of mulberries and citrus fruits. On the other hand, unlike today, flax was grown for fibre as well as seed, and not only in the Po valley but also further south; in the territory of Viterbo for example we read of a pond for retting flax.

It is obvious that the progress of cultivation, though as yet barely begun, and the general need to increase production for the urban market, must have made peasant farmers anxious to get their labour rents reduced and devote as much time as possible to working their own land. In this connexion it is interesting to notice how dependent cultivators in the countryside of Lucca were divided into two classes: the *angariales* who rendered heavy labour dues (usually three days a week), and the *redditales* who simply paid rent in money and kind. Of these it was precisely the peasants with holdings nearest the city who paid mere money rents or rents assessed in money.

The leases to peasants which give us reason to believe that some improvement, or at any rate change, had occurred in the condition of tenant cultivators, form only a small part of the contracts surviving from this period. Far more numerous, and far more disturbing to the system of landownership, were the grants made to tenants of higher social status, who did not personally work the land that they rented but let it out to others. Contracts of this kind ranged from leases for 29 years (*livelli*) to grants for one or three lives, *precariae*, and deeds of exchange. The beneficiary was sometimes an ecclesiastic, sometimes a small or middle-class proprietor, a feudal knight (*miles*) or count; very few were townsmen. What they commonly did was to grant some church or monastery a little land and money on purpose to receive back a much larger quantity of land in temporary use for any period up to three lives. Rents were nominal rents in money and only occasionally comprised small amounts of corn, as when grain-mills were granted with the land. According to some historians the object of these "remuneratorial leases", which preponderate among the records of the tenth century, was primarily political: they were granted, that is, to followers of the king or feudal lord to ensure their fealty and service. Other writers simply regard them as a means of rearranging and consolidating properties and tenures in units more convenient and rational to manage. But most people treat them as concealed alienations, and although the first two explanations may account for certain cases, there can be no doubt that most of these leases, on church land at least, were little more than sales in disguise. Indeed we have an unimpeachable authority for this opinion in Gerbert of Aurillac, later pope Sylvester II (999–1003), who on being chosen abbot of Bobbio was shocked to find that "by reason of certain documents (*codices*) called *libelli* the entire monastic patrimony had been granted away, so that nothing was left under his control". He complained further that the bishop of Pavia was treating ecclesiastical property as if it were his own, in order to reward his knights (*milites*). Gerbert therefore obtained a charter from the emperor Otto III abrogating all grants made by the abbots of Bobbio during the previous fifteen years. It was also laid down that, in future, *libelli* should only be granted to peasants (*laborantes*). Of similar tenor was an edict published by

64

Otto in 998 which limited all leases of church land, whether by emphyteusis or by *libellus*, to the term of one life. The practical result of these various measures hardly corresponded to the intentions behind them; but they certainly show that the process of alienation had been carried to disturbing lengths, and this suggests that more general economic causes were at work than the mere cupidity of abbots and bishops, causes arising from the progress of a money and exchange economy and increasing difficulties in the way of demesne farming. Although the documents rarely say so, it can be confidently assumed that much of the land which was granted away was in fact demesne land. In the tenth century the demesne was breaking up, and this was to lead, in the two centuries following, to the total collapse of the manorial system.

CHAPTER SIX

Italy in the Eleventh and Twelfth
Centuries

I. SOCIAL CHANGES AFTER THE TENTH CENTURY
AND THE RISE OF THE URBAN COMMUNES

THE changes in social life and organization which started to
appear in town and country during the tenth century gathered
speed in the century which followed and quickened to the pace
of crisis. On all sides we find evidence of ferment. In the past
most people had been satisfied to live their lives within the
narrow limits of a fief; but now they readily moved from place
to place in search of better things. Social relations were disturbed by protest and unrest in the lower classes, from whose
ranks a new middle class began to form and rise. Traditional
beliefs were suddenly challenged by an outbreak of mystical
heresies, which found their widest support once again among
the humbler classes. The crisis reached its climax in the late
eleventh and early twelfth centuries, when power passed in the
towns from the feudal overlord or bishop to organized groups
of citizens; while in the coutryside the mass of dependent
cultivators—or those at least who could advance some claims
to freedom—secured statutes defining their relations with the
lord, in place of the vague uncertain customs which up to that
time unscrupulous magnates had managed to manipulate for
their own advantage.

From a strictly economic point of view it used to be maintained that, in the case of the towns, this movement represented
the triumph of business capital over landed wealth, of commercial and artisan enterprise over agriculture, which up to then, it
was thought, had everywhere predominated. But in developing

this interpretation of the rise of urban communes, historians disregarded the first hundred years of communal history and considered only the great mercantile communes of the thirteenth and fourteenth centuries, where the middle classes had indeed by that time gained the upper hand and seized control of municipal government. This is not to deny that in certain towns of the middle Po valley, particularly Cremona and Milan, but also less conspicuously Piacenza and Pavia, fairly abundant records remain, as we have seen, of a class of *negotiatores*, probably merchants, who lived as full-time traders in the city and who still carried on with their business even after making money enough to buy land. According to Violante, the most recent and searching historian of Milanese society before the commune, it was the merchants, together with the justices and notaries, who formed the class described as "citizens" (*cives*) in the contest between the German emperor and the Milanese bishop Aribert. In this struggle the *cives* sided with the bishop and the greater feudatories (*capitanei*) against the powerful and more numerous class of lesser feudatories (*valvassores*), who had lately obtained from the Emperor, by the famous constitution "de feudis", an hereditary right to their fiefs and consequently full independence of the *capitanei*. When peace had been restored, as Violante rightly observes, the *cives* demanded and obtained a place of their own in the feudal hierarchy. What they and their rivals did, in fact, was to arrange to share all rights and powers "in common". And so, at the end of the eleventh century, the "commune" of Milan was founded, as an institution based on the collective exercise, by means of elected "consuls", of feudal powers which had been rendered "common". Despite the evident part played by the merchants, there is clearly nothing in these events to indicate the triumph of business over landed interests; it would be truer to speak of merchants buying their way into the middle class of landowners with the proceeds of trade. Indeed, we still find as late as the thirteenth century that the statutes of many communes, which were notable centres of commerce, impose a property qualification on candidates for election to the town councils. This is not to say that the revival of trade did not powerfully influence the formation of the communes, but only that the influence was mainly indirect.

The precocious development of urban autonomy in Italy was obviously due in part to the commercial activity which appears after the mid ninth century along the shores of the Adriatic and southern Tyrrhenian, and to the trading relations of the coastal towns with the interior. All this traffic occasioned more frequent regional contacts, stimulated urban markets, and intensified the demand for agricultural produce, which was required to feed the maritime cities and also sometimes to ship abroad. Urban markets encouraged the rise of urban communes by combining with other and often stronger influences, of a political and military character, to draw people from the surrounding countryside into the town, releasing them from manorial controls and granting them a new economic freedom. But in very few places before the thirteenth century did the urban economy support a class of merchants—and still more of artisans—powerful and numerous enough to take the lead in political conflict and seize hold of urban government. And even granting, as it seems we must, that certain Roman guilds survived in a few towns of Lombard Italy, as well as further south, their dependent status as *officia* or *ministeria*, subject to rigid supervision by the state, must have confined them to a secondary place in urban society and excluded them from playing any part in the creation of the communes. When the guilds began to re-emerge in great numbers, between the late twelfth and early thirteenth centuries, communal government was already fully formed and the guilds as yet enjoyed no share in it. It would rather seem that their revival was not the cause but the effect of the new corporate spirit, of which the commune itself was the first and most emphatic expression.

For a proper understanding of the profound economic revolution which led to the formation of the communes and the rise of a bourgeois class, we must therefore turn from the details of urban society to the wider perspective of feudal society, and consider changing conditions on the land and in the class relationships of the people living there.

During the barbarian and early feudal period very little land was freely alienable. Immense tracts of wood and pasture were the demesne property of the king. Other enormous properties were immobilized by ecclesiastical and monastic mortmain, and even lay estates were so encumbered by the complex hierarchy of tenure as to be rendered practically inalienable. Hardly more flexible were the relations of landlords and peasants: on the one hand the condition of slaves had been so transformed that few personal slaves any longer remained; on the other hand the strict bonds of contract had been slowly replaced by the bond of common custom, so that the great majority of peasant cultivators were by now reduced to the same equal condition of praedial serfs, tied to holdings which they could not leave but from which at the same time they could not be evicted. In this general paralysis of property, land could scarcely be regarded as a source of income; but the disability was not felt to be a serious burden so long as the scanty population, the superfluity of wood and pastures reserved to great landlords or assigned to common use, and the perpetual threat of barbarian violence and invasion, encouraged owners and peasants to collaborate in providing for their simplest needs and seek as little as possible from the world outside. But the greater security of rural life that resulted from the building of town and castle defences and from the local protection of feudal lords and bishops, and then, in the tenth century, the cessation of Arab and Hungarian attacks, and the final transformation of slaves into tenants with families and goods of their own—all this eventually made conditions so much less precarious for the peasant classes that very soon their numbers must have started to increase. Although statistics of every kind for this period are wanting, there are signs enough of a rise in population, beginning perhaps in the tenth century and then proceeding with rapid intensity in the three centuries after. The evidence is unanimous, whether we consider the numerous leases which require new farms to be built and land to be cleared; the sharing by two or three families of holdings previously worked by one; the growing frequency of leases, already numerous as we have seen in the ninth and tenth centuries, for planting vines and making other improvements; the many grants of land to groups of families to build and inhabit new castles; or the massive reclamation of woods and, somewhat later, the organization of engineering works for river-control, drainage of swamps and, last of all, for irrigation and inland navigation.

Meanwhile the dissolution of the great estates, especially the ecclesiastical estates, continued apace after the end of the tenth century. More and more land, particularly demesne land, was put to farm, so that the administrative unit of the manor, which by now had ceased to fulfil any economic purpose, fell to pieces; and between the manorial lords and their dependent cultivators was interposed a large and powerful class of wealthy or well-to-do leaseholders, who were barely distinguishable from the lesser feudal vassals. The first to suffer by the creation of this new class of landholders were the peasantry, who were now no longer controlled by a church or monastery or absent feudal lord, but worked under the eye of some grasping lessee on the make. And so we hear increasingly of protests against unjust exactions (*superimpositiones*) and "evil customs" (*malae consuetudines*), and of peasants quitting the land or trying by organized resistance and revolt to limit the authority of their new landlords and get their obligations fixed by charters of collective franchise.

The unrest among the peasant classes obviously contributed to the social instability which prepared the way for social revolution. But although they may have helped, it was not the peasantry who struck the first blow against the ancient feudal order; it was the far more powerful class of wealthy lease-holders and minor vassals, who by this time had achieved such independence of the great territorial lordships from which they held their land, as to be much more nearly owners than tenants of their estates. These were the men who, in 1035, were encouraged by the emperor Conrad II to revolt at Milan against the bishops and greater feudatories (*capitanei*). A few years earlier, in 1024, members of the same social class were probably responsible for the disturbances at Pavia, in which the royal palace, symbol of subjection to feudal rents and services, was burned to the ground. What they wanted more than anything was to be rid of all remaining limitations on the free alien-ability of their land; and this was virtually accorded them by the *Constitutio de feudis* issued, we have seen, in 1037 by Conrad II, whose ambition it was to curb the power of the bishops and *capitanei* of Milan. The *Constitutio* extended the right of hereditary succession to sub-vassals and transformed them into free proprietors, quit of all but the largely formal ties which bound them to the sovereign.

Freed at last of what had become an intolerable restriction, this middle class of landowners, domiciled in the town, shifted its interest away from the royal palace and the court of the feudal lord and turned towards the city, where the urban market offered them means of profitably employing their revenues, where artisan production was increasing, and where they enjoyed the advantage of solidarity with their peers. This was what happened at Milan, after the defeat of the *capitanei* and the restoration of peace with the bishop, and it was the same in many other places. The tenth-century charters of the Ottonian emperors, granting bishops jurisdiction over cities and their suburbs, already indicate a conflict of interests between the urban market and the last vestiges of subsistence economy on the land, and between the landowners established in the town and the great feudal lords, many of whom still kept their manors, castles, and jurisdictions in the countryside. The one ambition of the middle-class landowners, allied with the justices, notaries, and merchants owning land, was never again to fall under the power of the feudal magnates. United as they often were by ties of blood, they now formed a group apart, outside feudal society. Their interests bound them to the city, to the urban market and the cathedral church; and so we find them beginning to share, alongside the bishop, in urban administration and justice. Then later on, generally towards the close of the eleventh century or the beginning of the twelfth, when the sharpest struggle was over and they no longer needed the bishop or any other public official to represent them, they started to nominate their own representatives, the consuls, who gradually assumed entire control of the city and the defence of citizen interests. The election of these magistrates marked the formation of the Commune, the Commune in its first aristocratic phase, when it still combined the character of a private association protecting the interests of a clan or a class with that of a public institution representing the whole urban community.

2. THE FIRST CRUSADE AND THE MARITIME TOWNS OF ITALY

It was during these years of urban revolution, when the consular regime was being established in the towns of inland

and coastal Italy, that the steady recovery of Western Christendom against Islam was brought to a victorious conclusion by the great co-operative enterprise of the First Crusade. The retreat of Islam had started a century before with the Byzantine reconquest of Crete, Cyprus, and Antioch, and had then proceeded stage by stage with the Norman conquest of Sicily, the Pisan and Genoese wars on the coasts of Corsica, Sardinia, and the Balearics, and the advance of the Spanish *reconquista* as far as the Tagus. One effect of these successes was to restore control of the Mediterranean to Italy and her traders and to raise the maritime republics of Italy to the height of their prosperity and power. It may be true that the First Crusade recruited most support in France, the Rhineland, and the Norman states; but nothing would have come of the venture without the help of the towns, almost all Italian, which had a long tradition of relations with the Byzantine world, and commanded naval power and money. It was they which provided the transports and warships and many of the arms and siege engines, and it was they which advanced funds for equipping and feeding the troops, as well as often sending contingents of their own. For their collaboration they were afterwards repaid with ample commercial advantages and a share in the lavish spoils of war. And so it is often alleged, with evident malice and exaggeration, that the capital wealth of the Italian maritime cities was mainly based on booty; while the truth is that at Venice and Amalfi at least, and possibly at Genoa and Pisa also, commercial activity was already very intense throughout the eleventh century and many families were already rich. What gave these towns their new position of advantage was not plunder from war, but their astuteness in extracting privileges from the new Christian princes of the East, which were far more generous than the earlier concessions of Byzantines and Arabs, and their enterprise in founding numerous colonies along the coast of Syria and Palestine, with which they developed a lively and lucrative trade.

The first Italian towns to profit from the war were Genoa and Pisa, since the greater number of crusaders came from western Europe and naturally turned for aid to the ports of the upper Tyrrhenian. Neither town had previously played much part in trade with the eastern Mediterranean, but now they soon overtook both Venice and Amalfi, and for a short time even made their influence in that area supreme. For their sturdy support at the siege and conquest of Antioch, the Genoese were rewarded by the new ruler, Bohemund of Taranto, with the grant of thirty houses, a bazaar and a well. The Pisans were no less fortunate. They despatched a relief force of 120 ships during the siege of Jerusalem, and although the fleet arrived after the city had fallen, their help was still so opportune and welcome that the bishop of Pisa, who had joined the expedition, was created Patriarch of Jerusalem and also enfeoffed, as representative no doubt of his city, with an entire quarter in the port of Jaffa, which shortly became the principal centre of exchange between Palestine and the West. The Venetians, meantime, had been restrained from intervening in the Crusade by their good relations with the Byzantine emperor, who only recently, in 1080, had repaid them for their help against the Normans by granting them entry and preferential treatment in all the ports beneath his rule in Europe and Asia, and who did not hide his suspicion of the Latin occupation of former imperial territory. But after the capture of Jerusalem, and the privileges conferred on the Pisans and Genoese, the Venetians too realized the expediency of taking part, and in 1100 they sent a fleet of 200 vessels to Jaffa for the use of Godfrey of Bouillon. In return for this they were promised a church and a suitable site for a market in every city subsequently taken by the crusaders, and were also granted immunity from taxes and from the right of wreck throughout the Kingdom of Jerusalem.

3. THE ITALIAN COLONIES IN THE LEVANT

After the great naval expeditions which marked the contribution of the maritime cities to the First Crusade, Venice, Genoa, and Pisa continued to help the feudal armies in their conquest of the coastal towns that remained in enemy hands, and with every new victory they demanded and obtained new privileges. The result was that, during the first half of the twelfth century, numerous Venetian, Pisan, and Genoese colonies sprang up in almost all the seaboard towns of Syria and Palestine as well as certain inland towns close to the sea. These colonies were of a special character. Though not unlike the Phoenician colonies of old, they differed from them in being founded, not in strange uncivilized places, but in populous and flourishing cities, which they left substantially unchanged in both racial composition and economy. Sometimes the colonists were enfeoffed by the crusading princes with a quarter, or even, in a very few cases, with the whole of a town. More often the grant was limited to a single street, with a building for common use, a certain number of private houses, a warehouse (*fondaco*), church, bakery, mill, and baths. In the seaports a landing-stage was almost always added, and an open space for holding a market. Often too some cultivated land was granted beside the city walls.

The concession of land and houses should not be mistaken for evidence of any mass migration to the towns of the Levant by Venetians, Pisans, and Genoese. What mattered most to these Italians was to have control of places where they could freely and safely proceed with their business of buying and selling, loading, unloading, and storing wares, without disturbance from the local authorities or any rival powers. They also desired exclusive possession of a street providing access from the wharves reserved for their ships to their lodgings in the towns. And to guarantee their freedom from outside interference they obtained the right to be tried in all civil and commercial cases by their own magistrates according to the laws of their own country. All other privileges apart from these—the grants of land, churches and quarters of towns—had a purely financial character: only the feudal revenues from these properties were transferred to the Italian cities, while the householders, occupiers, and cultivators remained as before native Jews or Syrians. In course of time, however, as trade grew more intense, the floating population which thronged these quarters, whenever galleys and ships arrived from home and caravans from overland, was joined by groups of permanent emigrants, and true colonial settlements developed, comparable in every way to the European colonies founded in the great trading cities of the Far East during the later nineteenth century.

From the year 1104 we find the Italian colonies entrusted to the charge of magistrates called viscounts, bailiffs, or, more often, consuls, who had much more in common with the urban magistrates of their homeland than with the modern representatives of states abroad. They were not appointed simply to defend the commercial and other interests of their countrymen before the local authorities; they were the real governors of the colony, sometimes chosen by the residents themselves, sometimes sent from the mother country, but in either case quite independent of the local ruler and invested with all but total powers of jurisdiction, not only over their fellow citizens but also over the native population settled in the quarter or on the land granted to their city in fee.

The trade which developed in the Italian colonies of the twelfth century, scattered from Alexandretta to Jaffa, did not differ greatly in form or in the class of goods exchanged from the trade of Phoenicians, Greeks, and Romans in antiquity. Products of the Indies, Persia, and the Far East (pepper and other spices, perfumes, precious stones, silk) together with local merchandise, especially Syrian wares (cotton, silk, alum, arms, and other manufactures) were acquired in exchange for the few commodities the West had to offer (timber, metals, woollen cloth), or more often paid for with money or precious metals.

In later years, especially after the mid thirteenth century, we find Italian merchants following in the track of the first Christian missionaries and the pioneering Polos across the Asian continent as far as Mongolia and China. But normally, and in the early days particularly, they did not leave the coast, or if they did, it was only to visit the larger towns nearby, Aleppo, Antioch, and Damascus, and meet the caravans arriving overland from Mesopotamia, Arabia, India, Persia, and China.

It was not long before occasional ships were braving papal anathemas and moving down the coast from Syria and Palestine to the ports of Muslim Egypt, where the Italian merchants, though not so privileged yet as in the new Crusading states, could obtain the products of the Far East, India, and the Nile valley, at more reasonable price, because nearly all goods reached there by water. Even later, when the Holy Places had once more fallen to the Arabs and fresh crusades were launched to regain them, neither wars nor papal prohibitions ever brought this traffic to a complete stop. Alexandria remained as regular a destination of Italian ships and merchants as the ports of Palestine and Syria; indeed, it was mainly there that they bought the rich products arriving from the Indian Ocean.

In 1225 a few months' delay in the delivery of cargoes from Alexandria was enough to cause the price of pepper and other spices to rise sharply all over western Europe.

The coast of Africa west of Alexandria, or more exactly west of Tripoli, remained down to about 1200 the preserve of Pisans and Genoese. Only a few bold Venetian merchants ventured that way. But Pisans and Genoese maintained close relations with Tunisia, Algeria, and Morocco, which supplied the nascent cloth industry of the Tuscan towns with the famous "garbo" wool.

4. THE WESTERN OFFENSIVE IN THE BYZANTINE EAST

After the brief success of Godfrey of Bouillon the Crusades never again achieved their purpose of delivering the Holy Places from the Muslims. But their indirect results were not the less momentous. From the southern corner of Asia Minor as far as the straits of Gibraltar, a network of colonies had been created, which for more than three centuries made the maritime cities of Italy, and later also those of southern France and Catalonia, assured masters of Mediterranean commerce. A further effect, hardly less important, was to upset the traditional relations of the eastern Empire with the West. For the Crusades, which were planned by pope Urban II to bring help from Western Christendom to the Byzantine Empire in its struggle with the Arabs and Turks, had proved as serious a menace to the Greeks as the forces of Islam. The rising energies of western Europe, which had only just emerged from barbarism, were suddenly turned eastward, aggressive with ambition and greed. Near-Eastern territories, which had once belonged to the Empire and should have been restored to the Empire, were occupied by new crusading states, which lost no time in declaring their independence and hostility; while, inside the frontiers of the Empire, the maritime cities of Italy became increasingly self-assertive. At Constantinople itself the presumption and arrogance of the "Latins" provoked such bitter resentment that, in their effort to appease local feeling, the Emperors were forced to follow a vacillating policy, often in conflict with their interests, and try to exploit rivalries among the Italians themselves by granting to the Pisans and Genoese much the same privileges as those already granted the Venetians. The policy produced unwelcome effects. For one thing, it increased the number of Italians living in Constantinople, or visiting its port, to a total estimated by chroniclers of the later twelfth century at several tens of thousands; for another, it sharpened the dissension and violence between the Pisans and Genoese on the one hand and the Venetians on the other. Of these warring groups the Venetians were the most disliked by the people and the ruler of the eastern Empire; so much so, in fact, that in 1171 the order went out to arrest all Venetians resident at Constantinople and other cities of the Empire and sequestrate their goods. The lively reaction of Venice, supported by William II, king of Sicily, compelled the Emperor to reinstate the Venetians in their privileges and to promise compensation. But this only stirred up fresh hatred for the foreigner, and in 1182 a fearful riot broke out which ended in the capture and massacre of all Venetians and other Latins who had not fled. Twenty years later, in 1202, this violent hostility to the Latins, and especially the Venetians, met its due reward in the so-called Fourth Crusade, which was not a holy war against the infidel at all but an alliance for the conquest of Constantinople and the creation of a Latin Empire of the East (1204). The Crusade was a political triumph for the Venetians, who shortly before had been in danger of expulsion from the Aegean, but now at one stroke recovered their supremacy all along the coasts of the Empire; and this time they took care to build their power on far firmer foundations than mere imperial privilege. The treaty concluded by the doge Enrico Dandolo with the crusading leaders before the installation of the new Emperor, Baldwin of Flanders, granted Venice full dominion over three-eighths of all imperial territory, comprising the entire coast of the Ionian sea from Epirus to the southern tip of the Morea, Crete, Negropont and the principal islands of the Archipelago, Gallipoli and Adrianople in Thrace. In practice not all this territory became Venetian, for Venice had no army and could draw on no surplus rural population to support a policy of territorial aggrandizement. The Venetian government therefore renounced its rights on the mainland, and simply reserved a monopoly of trade and immunity from customs in the coastal areas to which it had claim, and which it agreed should be granted out instead to Greek or crusading feudatories. The only places actually occupied by the Venetians were certain strategic ports (Durazzo in Epirus, Modone and Corone in Morea), which were used as naval bases, and the islands, which were assigned after long and difficult conquest to members of the Venetian nobility. These nobles held on feudal terms, engaging to defend the islands and maintain them under Venetian sovereignty. In this way arose the feudal dynasties of the Sanudo lords of Naxos, the Dandolo of Andros, the Barozzi of Santorino, the Querini of Stampalia, and many more patrician houses who ruled their islands like true feudal lords, while at Venice itself they remained simple citizens, attending the sessions of the Maggior Consiglio, holding office in the normal way, and employing themselves in trade and shipping in common with all others of their class. The places of greatest strategic value, like Modone and Corone, were ruled directly by Venice, and the most important of the new dominions, the island of Crete, which attracted numerous immigrants, received a more complex organization: the land was parcelled out in fiefs to Venetian families, while the towns and ports became self-governing communities with the same institutions as Venice. At the same time the Venetian quarter at Constantinople was extended and became so populous that a second Venice seemed destined to develop there. The quarter was administered by a *podesta* or *bailo* who, apart from governing the colony, also acted as general representative of Venice in all her eastern possessions. Finally as regards commerce, the Venetians were guaranteed complete freedom of trade in all ports of the Empire. This gave them a manifest advantage over merchants from the other Italian cities, who, though never excluded from the markets at Constantinople and elsewhere, secured only mild reductions of customs duty. The sixty years of Latin rule at Byzantium truly represent the golden age of Venetian expansion in the East. But not all the profit went to Venice. During the same period Pisan and Genoese trade also flourished in Byzantine waters, despite Venetian privilege and the constant strife between the colonies of the rival towns.

And so, after nearly two hundred years of intense and arduous preparation, the thirteenth century opened a new period for all

the major maritime cities of Italy, the period of their greatest
conquests and greatest enterprise; and all this at once affected
the development of the towns in the interior.

5. ECONOMIC PROGRESS IN THE GREAT INLAND COMMUNES AND THE DEVELOPMENT OF THE BOURGEOISIE

The revival of urban life, of which we were able to study the
early phases in the eleventh-century towns of Lombardy, and
which was probably common to other towns of the Po valley
and Tuscany, had also spread during the eleventh and twelfth
centuries into southern Italy. Not only had many southern
towns risen to great prosperity; they had also become self-
governing, with officially recognized customs and even codes of
municipal law, and with the privilege of exercising jealously
guarded sovereign rights such as the right to coin money and
conclude commercial and political treaties. This rapid movement towards municipal liberties was brought to a stop by the
unifying and centralizing policy of Roger II, and then in the
thirteenth century suppressed outright by Frederic II, who
would tolerate no privileges of town or class incompatible with
royal authority. But even without opposition from the Crown
it may be doubted whether urban autonomy could have
flourished much longer in the south, for by the time of the early
Angevin rulers the evidence suggests that economic conditions
had ceased to favour the development of an urban class wholly
supported by trade and industry. In strictly formal terms, no
doubt, the urban commune was a creation of feudal society; it
came into existence with the transfer of certain public rights, by
sovereign concession, from a feudal lord to a group of vassals
associated for the purpose. In reality, however, this transfer of
rights was accompanied by a revolutionary change in society:
the formation and entry into politics of a bourgeois class.

The bourgeoisie emerges as a class in the first century of the
urban commune, or what is generally called the "consular"
period. During that time two complementary movements are
evident. On the one hand the commune invaded the countryside (*contado*) in order to protect its interests, and began to
extend its authority beyond the walls and suburbs of the town;

on the other a massive migration from the countryside invaded the town. The immigrants were of every kind. Some were minor feudal lords or simple landowners who, partly of their own free will but more often under duress, came to settle in the city, or engaged at least to build a house there and reside for certain months of every year, simultaneously renouncing all jurisdiction over their "subjects" (*homines*) in favour of the commune. More numerous were the free tenants (*libellarii*) and vassals of feudal lords in the *contado* who came without condition or constraint, either attracted by the nearby urban market or impatient to be free of feudal obligation. Immigrants of this class, it must be noted, did not normally sever all relation with their former life; most of them retained their land and connexions in the countryside. The case was otherwise with the class of dependent cultivators, the praedial serfs and slaves. For them the city, with its growing population and developing trades, offered not only increasing opportunities of work but also the promise of personal freedom, which most urban statutes were ready to grant at the end of a few years' residence. Migration for them, in short, meant greater security and the chance of a better paying occupation and more tolerable condition of life.

Before 1300 neither chronicles nor other sources permit us to measure even roughly the size of urban population. But they do offer unanimous proof of a very rapid increase in numbers, which between 1100 and 1250 must have raised the population of many Italian towns from a mere 5,000 or 6,000 souls to 30,000 and even more. An increase of this order is suggested particularly by the repeated extension of city walls, which in certain places came to include an area ten times larger than that within the original perimeter; and even then the space was often too narrow to contain the whole population, part of which spread outside into crowded suburbs. In these conditions the towns took on an entirely changed appearance. What had once been open field and pasture, swamp and waste, sparsely covered with huts of clay, wood, or wattle, an occasional rustic chapel and the barest scattering of public and ecclesiastical buildings, now became congested with the lowly wood and stone houses of the urban multitude, dominated here and there by the towered dwellings of immigrant nobles, majestic

Romanesque churches, and austere public palaces, which bore witness to the energy and ambition of the new burgess classes. No less radical were the changes in society and economic life. In the early days of the communal regime the economic links between town and country were still unbroken. The urban population was still quite small, and beside a few artisans and merchants, urban society was still composed of a certain number of clerks, justices, and notaries, and a group of middle-class landowners who had joined together and brought their dependent tenants under the control of the commune. At this time no doubt it was the custom of the humbler inhabitants, whether long-established residents or recent settlers, to go out each morning to work in the fields and come back each night, as people still do today in many towns of southern Italy. The proprietors and peasants whose home was in the towns lived mainly on the produce of their land, which they stored in ware-houses, cellars, and stables inside the walls. Only a part of their produce was intended for exchange with merchants and artisans in return for goods the land could not supply and household industry no longer provided insufficient quantity. But conditions were very different after the communes had subdued the lords of the *contado*. The economic unity of the manor, already compromised by the break-up and alienation of demesne, was now completely destroyed. Steadily the urban market extended its range and importance, manorial workshops disappeared or decayed, and even country people turned to the town for the goods they could not make at home. The growing demand of town and country for manufactured wares attracted a large number of immigrant countrymen into urban crafts; and in a short time slaves and serfs were transformed into free artisans. The final result of this process, at least in the more important places, was a sharp division of labour between country and town. The primary function of the country was to produce food and raw materials while the town became the centre of industry and trade.

At the same time immigration from the country had the effect of developing class distinctions in the towns. On the one hand an aristocracy grew up composed of great landowners; these men were wedded to the past and had no wish to sacrifice their traditional immunities, their share in public revenues, or the rights they enjoyed over subject *homines* who had now become members of the commune. On the other hand were all those men who had entered some urban trade or profession and cut the ties which bound them to the court of their feudal lord; their wish was to be free of all ancient claims to rent and services and to exercise their chosen trade in peace. The merchant class occupied an intermediate position, formed as it was not of simple shopkeepers retailing goods from stalls in the town square, but of citizens who travelled long distances to foreign fairs and markets and imported merchandise from abroad. In a few towns, where commerce had developed most rapidly, we find the merchants owning land and taking part in communal government from the very beginning, alongside the landed aristocracy. But more often we find them leading the urban artisans in their movement of association, resistance, and revolt, and providing the main strength of the new middle class, or what was then called "The People" (*popolo*).

6. ORIGIN, CHARACTER, AND PURPOSE OF THE CRAFT AND MERCHANT GUILDS

During the second half of the twelfth century we begin to hear of artisans and merchants being organized in what today are usually described as trade and professional guilds, but in the towns of medieval Italy were variously known as *arti*, *fraglie*, *paratici*, and so on. The guilds included not only the masters of each trade but also, in a subordinate position, their working companions (*socii*, *laborantes*) and apprentices (*discipuli*).

In recent times, as we have seen, and especially since the publication of the *Honorantiae civitatis Papiae*, most historians have accepted the conclusion that, at least in certain towns of medieval Italy both Byzantine and Lombard, some kind of guild organization had continued to exist in a number of trades which engaged in work of importance to the state; such guilds paid dues to the government and were granted rights of monopoly in return. But, in spite of these relics from the past, the evidence leaves no doubt that the twelfth-century guilds were new institutions, created by conditions which only developed in the urban communes after their first foundation and after the influx of people from the country. One sign of this is the sudden and rapid rise of guilds in the second half of the twelfth century. Another is the form, which the guilds first assumed, of perfectly free associations. A final proof is the growth of similar corporations, about the same time, in towns of central and north-west Europe which had never been more than faintly influenced by the ancient Roman world. Indeed if the few artisans and merchants who lived in the towns of the tenth and earlier centuries had all been combined in close, monopolistic guilds of the kind revealed by the *Honorantiae*, they would surely have put up a bitter fight to keep out new competitors from their trades and organization. It is far more likely that the initiative came from the former feudal subjects (*homines*) of lords in the *contado*, who after moving to the town and adopting some new craft or trade, felt the need to draw together in common defence against their ancient masters. It is no doubt possible that they were influenced by surviving Roman traditions and by the example of guilds already established in the town. Nor can it be said for certain that the new corporations were quite unaffected by the long tradition of manorial workshops, where slaves were divided into groups under masters (*magistri*) according to their several crafts (*ministeria*). But more than anything they were governed by the universal impulse of their time to unite in sworn associations of defence and defiance, like the clan federations of nobles (*consorterie, Società delle Torri*), the armed companies of commoners (*compagnie armate del popolo*), the religious confraternities of pious laymen, and—most important of all—the urban commune itself. From the commune, specifically, the craft and merchant guilds borrowed their form of organization.

Economic causes, however, were hardly less important. The very custom of the urban market encouraged combination, for by ancient tradition all tradesmen practising the same craft produced and sold their goods in shops on the same street. This is why so many streets, especially round the markets of old Italian towns, bear the name of particular trades: Smith St. (Via dei Fabbri), Baker St. (Via dei Pistori), Weaver St. (Via dei Tessitori), and so on. Guilds in fact were not established simply to protect artisans from the insolence of aristocratic *consorterie*; for this purpose they could probably rely on the armed companies, which were formed about the same time in the ranks of the urban *popolo*. The function of the guilds was economic as much as social. In particular they met the needs of an urban economy which could only command a closed and limited market. The market was limited because the communes were so numerous. One after another, in the space of a few decades, all the ancient Roman cities which had survived the ruin of the Empire, as well as many of the larger *castelli*, developed into self-governing communes, bent on asserting their political and economic supremacy throughout the surrounding countryside. The number of towns all over north and central Italy which achieved practical autonomy in the course of the twelfth century was astonishingly high. As a result the average distance separating one commune from another never exceeded 20 to 25 miles, so that even after the *contado* had been wholly subjugated, the conquered territory never reached much further than 10 to 12 miles from the city walls. To go beyond was to enter foreign and unfriendly country. For, despite occasional treaties of good neighbourship, which may have encouraged reciprocal trade, most communes lived in a state of undeclared or open warfare with bordering states. Only in the season of fairs, when special safe-conducts were in force, could the citizens of any commune venture across the frontier for purposes of trade; otherwise they might forfeit their goods and often their liberty as well.

In these conditions it was natural to try to organize production in such a way that town and country could provide as far as possible for all their basic and reciprocal needs. And so it became a matter of policy to maintain inside the city a multitude of small specialized industries, each of which was restricted to so small a clientele that they would infallibly have gone out of business had not measures been introduced to check competition between men of the same trade and prevent any fatal crisis of overproduction. Rules were therefore adopted to govern the relations of masters and workmen, limit the number of apprentices, and fix their period of training. Sharp penalties were imposed on masters who hired runaway workers or raised wages above the statutory limit. Outsiders were inhibited from practising established trades but tempted with favours to introduce trades that were new. The acquisition and use of raw materials was minutely regulated to ensure high quality. Methods of sale were controlled and price-lists circulated. And many days of the year were set aside for compulsory rest.

By its very nature a system so nicely balanced that every petty trader and artisan could calculate the exact demand of his few, unchanging customers, was certain to break down as soon as economic enterprise in some of the larger towns outgrew the narrow limits of the early commune. But this development, which was destined to transform the social and economic structure of the larger cities, only took place during the second period of communal history, especially after the first decades of the thirteenth century and in the first half of the fourteenth, when the urban economy of medieval Italy may be said to have entered its prime.

CHAPTER SEVEN

The Urban Economy in its Prime
The Thirteenth and Fourteenth Centuries

I. THE EXPANSION OF THE GREATER MARITIME CITIES AFTER THE FOURTH CRUSADE

DURING the century following the First Crusade, we have seen that the maritime cities of Italy secured very favourable conditions for their commerce in the eastern Mediterranean by the privileges granted their trading-stations in various towns of the Crusading States. After the Fourth Crusade and the foundation of the eastern Latin Empire this privileged position was transformed into unconditional supremacy.

Those who benefited most, as we have seen above, were the Venetians, until at last, in 1261, the Genoese got their revenge by helping Michael Paleologus to recapture Constantinople. But just as the Venetian victory of 1204 did not prevent the Pisans and even less the Genoese from trading in the Levant, so the Genoese counter-stroke of 1261 disturbed Venetian power much less than might have been expected. The Venetians lost their privileges, but they retained their valuable bases at Modone and Corone and most of the Aegean islands. Above all they kept Crete, which was of cardinal importance, not only to the fleets visiting Egypt, Syria, and Palestine, but also for its agricultural produce. Constantinople remained a centre of business for Venetian merchants, shippers, and bankers, and also served as a starting-point for Venetian trading-vessels travelling to the Black Sea. In that sea, which the Latin offensive against Byzantium had first thrown open to western merchants, the Venetians not only frequented such ports of the southern coast

86

as Trebizond, where regular caravans arrived from the Persian Gulf, but also followed the Genoese on to the northern coast, where they founded a colony at Tana, at the mouth of the Don in the Sea of Azov. Tana was important as a centre for trade with southern Russia, and also offered access to the markets situated in the Volga delta and beyond the Caspian Sea.

The value to Genoa and Venice of their conquest of eastern markets must be measured by the quality much more than the quantity of merchandise brought home. A few figures soon make this clear. At Venice, in the fourteenth century, the entire cargo of eastern wares could normally be carried by three state convoys or *mude*, travelling once every year to their separate destinations at Constantinople (and the Black Sea), Beirut, and Alexandria. Each convoy comprised two to four galleys, and the burden of the largest merchant galleys rarely exceeded 500 tons in the thirteenth century, possibly less. Of this tonnage barely one-third was ever free for cargo, since space had to be found for over 60 oarsmen, 20 or more crossbowmen, a good number of officers, mates, and merchants, and often a company of pilgrims as well, besides food and water for the journey. The necessary conclusion seems to be that all the Venetian ships together can have transported only some 2,000 tons of merchandise from the East. And things were no different at Genoa. In certain years, it is true, when a larger quantity of goods was expected on the quays of the Levantine ports, permission was granted for the surplus wares to be loaded in unarmed vessels. Moreover, about the middle of the fourteenth century, we begin to hear of the so-called "cotton convoy", bound for the ports of Cyprus, Armenia, and Syria, and composed of rounded sailing-ships, which had a much greater capacity than galleys. With these additions we might reach an annual total of 5,000 tons.

To some extent the modest size of these eastern cargoes was balanced by their value, which early fifteenth-century chroniclers sometimes estimate at 200,000 ducats for every galley. But far more remunerative was the custom they attracted to those markets which were able to supply them in sufficient quantity. The precious commodities of the East drew merchants from all over the Italian hinterland and the countries beyond the Alps, in particular Germany. They were also re-exported by the Italian merchants themselves, first by land and then

87

increasingly by sea, after Venice and Genoa started sending Atlantic convoys to Flanders and England.

In sheer quantity and bulk oriental wares were far surpassed by certain primary products of general consumption, pre-eminently salt and grain. For trade in salt Venice was much better situated than Genoa, which had to fetch supplies from Sardinia, the Balearics, and the African coast, and even then could only get them to inland markets by using road transport over the Apennines. Venice, by contrast, had been able for centuries to draw on saltworks in and round the city, and although these were now exhausted and dry, salt in abundance could easily be got from the no less productive works of Chioggia and Istria, and if they proved insufficient, from the saltpans of Romagna, Apulia, Sardinia, the Balearics, Tripolitania, and Cyprus. With such resources, Venice was able to supply not only its own dense population but the whole Po valley as well, using river transport, which was cheaper than transport by land. Considering the enormous demand for salt, which was needed not only for men but also for cattle, we can easily see that several hundred tons must have been imported by sea, while hundreds of private craft were steadily employed bringing cargoes of salt across the Mediterranean and Adriatic, and as many barges were engaged in transporting it across the Lagoon and up the rivers of Venetia and the northern plain.

Almost as great in quantity, and certainly greater in value, were the cargoes of seaborne wheat. Venice had even less land than Genoa to feed its population, which had rapidly increased since the twelfth century. Yet it is perfectly plain from records of the fourteenth and fifteenth centuries that Venice was one of the cities most lavishly provided with foodstuffs. In normal years the demand for wheat and other grains could be met in part by imports from the states of the northern plain, more particularly perhaps Ferrara and Mantua. But at the slightest threat of famine or war, the inland communes hurried to enforce their food restrictions and forbid all export of grain. And so Venice, like Genoa, was largely dependent on regular shipments by sea. These overseas supplies came partly from Romagna, the Marches, and the Abruzzi, but mostly from Apulia, and later on, during the Angevin and Aragonese period, from Sicily as well. Corn exports from these two southern provinces were encouraged by the fiscal needs and policy of the Crown; for the kings of Naples and Sicily obtained considerable revenue from the sale of export licences or *tratte*, most of which in consequence went to the towns with most money: Genoa, Venice, and, during the Angevin period, Florence also. Venice, however, did not rely exclusively on Italian sources of supply, but also drew quite large amounts from abroad, sometimes from Crete and Egypt, more often from the Balkan peninsula (upper and lower Rumania) and the Black Sea ports. Altogether the yearly corn imports of Venice were so considerable that it must have needed dozens and dozens of small and medium-sized ships to carry them. And the government was usually able not only to stock the granaries with large reserves, but also to grant permission for export to many lords and towns of the mainland, some of them a long distance away.

Two other imports which helped appreciably to increase the activity of private shipping were wine and oil. Both were procured mainly in the Adriatic ports from Ravenna southwards, as well as in Crete, the Morea, and the islands of the Aegean; and they were re-exported to the mainland, subject to government licence, even more regularly than grain.

The great Italian sea powers of the western coast of Italy never managed to control the Tyrrhenian as Venice controlled the Adriatic; instead they had to suffer competition from the towns of Provence and then, even worse, from the Catalans and Aragonese. Their number also declined. Only two were left when Amalfi decayed, and finally only one, when the Genoese victory at Meloria, in 1284, completely destroyed the political if not the commercial power of Pisa.

Before Meloria, however, the Pisans exercised predominant influence from the mouth of the Magra to Monte Argentario. They controlled the Tuscan archipelago and shared with the Genoese dominion over Corsica and Sardinia. Led by their bishop, they played an energetic part in the First Crusade. Numerous Pisan colonies were planted in Syria and Egypt, Tunisia and Algeria, and large numbers of Pisan merchants frequented the Balearics, the eastern coast of Spain, and the towns of southern France. The trade of Pisa was partly nourished by imports of salt, grain, iron, and silver from the Italian territory under Pisan rule or influence, and partly by the manufactures of the Pisan woollen industry. But more than anything Pisa owed its commercial importance, even after Meloria, to its function as the local port of Lucca and the centre of imports and exports for Tuscany and the Tuscan-Emilian Apennines. Merchants of Florence, Lucca, Prato, and other Tuscan towns travelled with their merchandise on Pisan ships, and on Pisan ships they imported goods from the Levant, Africa, and Spain, which were brought from Porto Pisano to the towns inland. For this reason Pisa developed a much larger carrying trade than other maritime cities.

In some things Genoa resembled Pisa, being poor in territory, poorer even than Pisa, and producing very few crops or manufactured goods for home consumption or trade. At the same time the commercial hinterland of Genoa was far more ample and rich, despite the intervening Apennines, which were low and narrow and easy to cross. It embraced the whole of Lombardy, with western Emilia, the plain of Piedmont and the Italian parts of Switzerland, and extended across the Alpine passes of the Little St. Bernard, the Septimer and the St. Gotthard into Germany, Switzerland, the Rhineland, and eastern France. The scope of Genoese trade and seapower in the Mediterranean became correspondingly wide after the Crusades, and especially after the restoration of the Greek Empire in 1261. Previously, Genoese commerce had been limited to the northern Tyrrhenian; but after the late eleventh century it rapidly spread to Sicily, Malta, and the coasts of Barbary and the Magreb. Here the Genoese founded numerous colonies, sometimes in collaboration but more often in competition with the Pisans. Further colonies were established after the First Crusade, in Syria and Palestine, and, after 1261, on the shores of the Aegean, the Sea of Marmora, and the Black Sea. Supported by a mighty mercantile marine and protected by a powerful navy (which profited by conditions of persistent war to engage in large-scale piracy), Genoese trade developed an enormous range, extending from the Crimea to the Straits of Gibraltar and eventually, after the late thirteenth century, to the ocean routes beyond. As a result, Genoa became the centre of a flourishing market, attracting crowds of merchants from northern Italy. The most

frequent visitors at first were traders from the towns just north
of the Ligurian Apennines, in particular Novi, Tortona, Asti,
and Piacenza; but these were followed in time by even larger
numbers of merchants from Milan, who came to form a thriving
colony in the city. The Milanese imported metals and metalwork in iron and steel, supplemented later by large quantities of
woollen cloth; in exchange they exported northward, from
Genoa, as from Venice, such products as pepper and other
spices, wax, cotton, dyestuffs, and wool.

Genoese trade probably reached the peak of its rapid rise in
the last ten years of the thirteenth century. At that time more
people lived in Genoa than at any other period before the
eighteenth century, not counting numerous settlers from all over
the world, many of whom sought rights of citizenship. A century
later, however, Genoa had started to decline, weakened by
internal discord and by the continual conflict with Venice
which culminated in the disastrous War of Chioggia in 1378–81.
From this war, which seemed at one time to threaten the total
destruction of Venetian power and independence, Genoa
emerged too feeble and exhausted to profit by the final peace
at Turin (1383); and within a few years the city had ceased
altogether to play a leading part in Mediterranean politics.
Nevertheless, as we shall see, individual Genoese remained as
active and enterprising as ever, and many became pioneers in
the exploration of the African coasts, patronized by the royal
court of Portugal.

2. ECONOMIC CONDITIONS IN THE GREATER COMMUNES
OF INLAND ITALY DURING THE THIRTEENTH AND
FOURTEENTH CENTURIES

The economic activity of the maritime cities, though certainly
not responsible for the rise of communes in the towns of the
interior, undoubtedly exercised a powerful influence on their
development after the twelfth century.

As we have said, in strictly formal terms the urban commune
can be considered a creation of feudal society; it came into
existence with the transfer of certain public rights, by sovereign
concession, from a feudal lord to a group of vassals associated

for the purpose. But in practice this transfer of power was encouraged and often caused by the revival of the towns as centres of exchange and the consequent formation of a bourgeois class.

One effect of the immigration already noted (p. 80) was a sharp and general increase in urban population, an increase described by several of the chroniclers, and illustrated, we have seen, by the steady enlargement, often on a massive scale, of the walled urban perimeter. Many towns must have trebled their population in little more than a century. Inside the walls new public buildings and churches, often of enduring beauty, shared the crowded space with the towered palaces of the immigrant nobility and the wood and stone hovels of the common people.

Side by side with this renovation and expansion of the city, changes of equal magnitude developed in society and economic life. In particular the subjugation by the commune of the lords of the *contado* destroyed once for all the vestiges of economic unity on manors and fiefs, and widened increasingly the range of urban markets. As the last manorial workshops began to disappear, even rustics had to turn to urban industry for what they could not make themselves. And so in Italy the political division of town and country was cancelled and replaced by an almost complete economic division of labour, whereby the country supplied food and raw materials and the towns practised trade and industry. Inside the city, however, divisions of a different kind appeared, in the growth of class distinctions. On the one hand an aristocracy arose composed of great land-owners, jealous for their ancient immunities, their share in public revenues, and all their traditional rights over dependent *homines*; on the other hand were the dependants themselves, who had entered some urban trade or profession and would tolerate no claims to ancient rent and services. But more important for urban history was the fact that, in between the old landed aristocracy and the manual workers who had turned from agriculture to industry, stood another class, the merchants; and the merchants were not mere shopkeepers selling goods from stalls in the *piazza*, but—in those communes at least where they formed an organized class—consisted of men of wealth and substance, engaged in foreign trade and travel and in the import of merchandise which the local town and territory were unable to produce. Merchants of this type were the natural leaders of the new middle classes, and in some communes we already find them sharing power with the nobles in the period of consular rule. As industry and trade intensified, they were quickly joined by other groups, not indeed by the mass of manual workers, but by the master craftsmen of the richer and more powerful guilds, which had been established in most cities of north and central Italy in the later twelfth century. In combination with the lesser merchants, who had not yet entered the nobility, the wealthier guildsmen came to form what was known in every town as "the people" (*popolo*), a middle-class alliance, which during the thirteenth century began to gain control of the commune.

As the government passed increasingly under middle-class influence, economic policy conformed increasingly to middle-class interests, interests, however, which were often common to the urban population at large. But what served the city did not serve the country. On the contrary the rural population was now subjected to a policy of systematic exploitation for the benefit of consumers and producers in the town. It is perfectly true that, by suppressing many feudal rights and freeing the class of serfs, the towns had contributed, directly or indirectly, to improving social conditions in the countryside. But when the feudal lords had been deprived of power, the towns simply took their place and proceeded to treat the country like colonial territory, as a source of food and a market for manufactures. In accord with this policy attempts were made to prevent households in the country from making goods produced in the towns. More revealing still, laws were introduced forbidding peasants to "fly" the land, the effect of which was to revive in favour of urban landlords a condition little different from the old praedial servitude.

Another matter which closely affected the economic relations of town and country was the food policy pursued by the urban communes. One supreme concern of all municipal governments was to avoid any shortage of food or rise in the cost of living, which would lead to a demand for higher wages. In years of abundant harvest the problem hardly arose, for even the towns with the densest industrial population and the least adequate supply of home-grown food could easily import corn and other basic produce from less populous regions nearby. But in years of scanty harvest the barriers were raised relentlessly between each commune and the next. And so, to avert the misfortune of too frequent famine, special officials were appointed (called officials of the *annona, grascia,* or *abbondanza*), whose task it was to study the periodic census of all persons above the age of infancy, check the local stocks of grain, estimate the need of the following year, and determine the measures to meet it. Then, on the bases of their calculations, the commune or prince proceeded to purchase large quantities of corn, if possible from neighbouring states which were not threatened with shortage, but more often from one of the maritime cities, which imported it mainly, as we have seen, from the Maremma, Apulia, Sicily, and the Byzantine East.

This dependence on food supplies from outside was one reason why the urban economy, in the larger towns at least, ceased to be a closed system in which town and territory could combine as a self-sufficient community. But other reasons were no less important. Thus the massive development of particular industries in different towns led to local specialization and reciprocal trade. At the same time a number of inland towns, where merchants had managed to accumulate substantial capital, began to play a part in international commerce. As early as the twelfth century numerous merchants of Asti, Chieri, Piacenza, Lucca, and Siena, were in the habit of visiting markets in southern France, Paris, and Champagne. Not long after, we find them also in London and Bruges. In all these places the Italians took up banking as well as trade, partly encouraged by the popes, who often made them agents for the transmission of papal taxes. Many were simply pawnbrokers, known collectively in northern towns as "Lombards", who did a thriving business in petty loans on small security. But some became financiers to princes and monarchs, great feudal lords and prelates. The bankers of Lucca, Siena, and particularly Florence, were the principal creditors of kings. The risks involved were certainly great, but so were the advantages obtained in the export of merchandise and the farm of customs and other revenues.

Among the towns most actively engaged in this mercantile

enterprise of the twelfth and thirteenth centuries were certain communes of northern Italy, in particular Asti and Piacenza, Cremona and Milan. From the twelfth century on, we find merchants and bankers of Asti at work in France, Burgundy, and England; they formed a primary group among the so-called "Lombards", who gave their name to the street still occupied by many of London's principal banks. Piacenza, which remained a centre of banking business down to the early seventeenth century, became commercially important because of its position at the junction of the Po with several busy highways: the Via Francigena (which led from England and France to Lucca, Siena, and Rome), the Via Emilia, and one of the main roads from Genoa to Milan. Cremona was another notable trading city on the Po, distinguished especially in the Middle Ages for its unrivalled fustian industry. The greatest town of all, however, was Milan, which after the decline of Pavia became the leading centre of trade and industry throughout the whole of Lombardy and the valley of the Po. Milan was already strong enough to rouse the jealousy of its neighbours in the early twelfth century. At the time of the struggle with the Emperor Barbarossa the merchants of Milan already possessed an organization with consuls of their own. And after the defeat of Barbarossa (1176) the Milanese gave further proof of their resource and wealth by starting to build the canals, drainage and irrigation works, to which lower Lombardy has ever since owed most of its prosperity. About the same period a woollen industry developed in the city, with help from the Umiliati brotherhood, and very soon it was producing abundant cloth for export. The most famous Milanese industry, however, was metallurgy, and especially the manufacture of arms.

Industry flourished also in the larger communes of Venetia, particularly Verona and Padua. The main commodity produced for export was woollen cloth. But not only trade was lucrative; in Dante's day we also hear of wealthy capitalists who engaged in moneylending on a very large scale. From time to time both Padua and Verona managed to extend control over great part of the Veneto, especially after the late thirteenth century, when the two towns were ruled by despotic families, the Scaligeri and Carraresi; but local rivalries and the jealousy of two great neighbouring powers, Venice and Milan, prevented them from ever establishing a durable dominion.

In Emilia, by contrast, none of the various urban communes scattered at regular intervals along the Emilian Way seriously disturbed the local balance of power during this period. Bologna, it is true, had particular advantages. It surpassed the other towns in industrial development. It also occupied a favoured position at the junction of the Via Emilia and the road from Venice to Florence and Lucca. In those days, moreover, it commanded access by water to the Po and the sea, which it later lost because of changes in the river system of the region. And finally the University, which was famous throughout Europe, drew people and trade to the town. But for all that, Bologna never developed so large a population or so great a surplus of production as to be impelled to undertake territorial conquest.

The first town in Tuscany to attain more than local economic importance was Lucca. Lucca was also the first town in upper Italy to engage in the manufacture of silk. For more than a century the Lucchese silk industry maintained an unchallenged supremacy; and when political unrest drove many of the merchants and craftsmen into exile, Lucca became inadvertently responsible for the growth of similar industries in Florence, Bologna, Venice, and Genoa. But the business men of Lucca had always been merchants rather than manufacturers, and as merchants they occupied a leading position in the trade of western Europe, and especially France, right down to the beginning of modern times.

Roughly contemporary with the rise of Lucca, though rather different in form, was the economic development of Siena. One source of Sienese wealth was mining, which was practised on a very large scale (for those days) in various parts of the wide Sienese dominion. But the main source was commerce. Siena was the meeting-place of two main roads to Rome: the Via Francesca from Piacenza and Lucca, and the road from Bologna and Florence. Such a situation not only favoured trade; it also encouraged frequent intercourse with the capital of Christendom, and this no doubt explains why pope Gregory IX chose Sienese merchant-bankers to collect the crusading tenth in the countries north of the Alps. The commission served the Sienese well; for it enabled them to increase their trade with the northern countries, and also probably their banking activity. Banking in fact was the main concern of the great Sienese families, who made their fortune during the thirteenth century—the Bonsignori and the Piccolomini, the Salimbeni and the Tolomei. Too often, however, these fortunes built on banking proved precarious. Loans to the popes and to foreign nobles, prelates, and princes, tied up so much capital that in the second half of the thirteenth century many Sienese houses, including the most powerful and famous of them all, the Tavola dei Bonsignori, went irredeemably bankrupt. The result was that the Sienese finally lost their dominant position in the Tuscan banking world to the great business companies of Florence, which had secured and distributed their capital better, by investing in larger and richer rural estates and exploiting a rapidly expanding industry.

The rise of Florence to supremacy in Tuscany occupied the best part of two hundred years, and as late as the mid thirteenth century the city was still closely encircled by independent urban communes and powerful feudal lords. Florentine wealth was derived from commerce, combined from an early stage with industry. Chief among the trade corporations (*Arti*) of the town was the guild of the Calimala merchants, so called from the street where they had their shops. The principal business of these merchants was the importation of French, Flemish, and English cloth; but since their trade involved them in close relations with countries abroad, they often engaged in banking as well, though at first on a limited scale. More important in the thirteenth century was the industry they developed for processing northern textiles to suit the taste of markets at home and in the Levant, to which they re-exported the dyed and finished cloth by way of Pisa, Venice, and later also Fano.

Quite independent of the Calimala guild was the purely industrial clothmakers' guild, or *arte della lana*, which by the early fourteenth century administered the greatest industry in Florence and possibly in the whole of Italy. At that time, according to the chronicler Giovanni Villani, the looms of Florence were producing more than 100,000 pieces yearly, though only of moderate quality; thirty years later, the same authority tells us, production had dropped by about one-third, but had so

97

improved in quality that the finer cloth, intended mainly for export, was fetching a price equal to or above that of the most highly prized fabrics of Flanders or France.

Long before this, however, the position which Florentine merchants had reached in the markets of western Europe was vividly revealed and powerfully strengthened by the gold coinage issued by Florence, concurrently with Genoa, in the year 1252. This coin was introduced in order to replace the Byzantine *hyperperon*, which had served as international currency for all Christian countries down to the twelfth century, but had then been rapidly and seriously debased. In the event the florin was far more successful than the Genoese coin or *genoino*, and it soon placed Florence in the front rank of the financial powers of Europe. But its triumph was not so much the cause as the measure of Florentine influence, and this was due to the great expansion of Florentine business in the markets of France, England, and the Low Countries, Rome and southern Italy, and even, to some extent, the Orient as well.

3. AGRICULTURE, INDUSTRY, AND TRADE IN THE AGE OF THE COMMUNES

a. Agriculture

The rise to predominance of the urban communes was accompanied by profound, indeed revolutionary, changes in the state of rural property; and these changes reacted in turn upon agriculture. The very vicinity of the towns, with their rapidly growing population, industry, and trade, was enough to disturb and disrupt the old manorial organization. Little by little were relaxed the ties of common interest which bound subject holdings to the lord's demesne and maintained cohesion and balance in the working of the great estates. The demand for labour rose, as more land was needed for tillage and tracts of waste were cleared which hitherto had only provided men with game or fish, wild marsh grasses, or a little rough grazing for pigs and other animals. Between the eleventh and the thirteenth centuries vast areas in the lowlands of the Po valley were drained, dyked, and reclaimed from wood, swamp, and waste. In the territory of Mantua, which has been studied in particular detail, the northward advance of the Po down to about 1100 necessitated the construction of elaborate embankments to protect the land abandoned by the river; the works are mentioned in many leases of the period, which require tenants to keep the banks in good repair. At the same time a spirited attack was begun on the woodland, pasture, and fen, which before the eleventh century had occupied most of Mantuan territory (in 1072 one large estate in the lowlands of Mantua comprised no less than 3,000 *jugera* of wood, beside a mere 32 *jugera* of cultivated land). It appears that the most effective means of carrying out this work, was to break up the greater properties into smallholdings and tenures. We find the same in the Polesine, the lowlands of Verona, and all the country lying along the Po and Adige: land at one time undivided and almost wholly desolate now became covered with farms. In some cases the transformation was the result of intensive and systematic colonization. Thus, during the years 1077 to 1091, the margrave Boniface of Canossa parcelled out his property into 233 separate holdings (*mansi*) of 10 *jugera* each, and let them to families of peasants on terms designed to promote the clearance of wood, the reclamation of waste, and most of all the planting of vines. The effect of such works on the countryside was well summed up in 1233 by the provost of Mantua cathedral, when he said that in less than a hundred years the lands of his church had been entirely "cleared, ploughed, redeemed from wood and marsh, and converted to the production of food (*ad usum panis reductae*)".

In cases like these the interests of landlords and peasants combined to hasten the break-up and disappearance of the old demesne; labour services were abandoned, and in their place tenants were required to co-operate in building dykes, developing new crops, and making other improvements. In other cases, however, the owners of great estates, especially church estates, were obliged to grant out land or demesne, which they could no longer work themselves, to tenants who were neither peasants nor cultivators. The grants were variously made by fief, emphyteusis, or *libellus* for 29 years; but whatever their type, they were all in reality concealed alienations: *dominium utile* became quite separate from *dominium directum*, and the tenant obtained unrestricted control of the land in return for payment of an insignificant rent.

Not all changes in the rural order were so obedient to the forms of law. Peasants in particular adopted more revolutionary methods. Often they simply refused to go on rendering dues and services which hindered them from giving full time to their holdings and exploiting the growing market for agricultural produce. Their resistance was usually successful and led to the conclusion of written agreements, which fixed the relations of landlord and tenant, suppressed all arbitrary exactions, and reduced all services to a minimum. These collective contracts served as the basis of later village statutes. All the same, collaboration did not cease between peasants and proprietors; sufficient proof of this is the steady diffusion of partiary tenure, which in most of central Italy and much of the Po valley came to assume the form of strict *métayage* or *mezzadria*. At the same time, the social character of landownership was itself largely transformed by the rise of a bourgeois class of landlords. This was partly the result of migration to the town by large numbers of rural proprietors, but partly due also to the tendency of merchants, grown rich by trade, to invest a proportion of their profits in land, for reasons of security or social prestige.

It was long believed that the Italian communes caused far more radical changes than these in the agrarian regime. In particular, they were said to have reformed the legal and social condition of the peasantry so completely that, five hundred years before the French Revolution, the labouring classes became perfectly free. With very good reason this opinion has been frequently criticized, or at any rate seriously qualified. To be sure, it was almost a general rule for rustics, who settled and lived in the city for a specified length of time, to be treated as free by the law; but the measures of collective enfranchisement which certain communes enacted were simply conceived as a means of fighting feudatories in the *contado*, and were never designed to overturn the foundations of rural society. While slavery disappeared entirely from the countryside, the ties which bound dependent peasants to the land were never effectively suppressed. The ties were no longer legal, but in practice most peasant cultivators (now called *villani*, *manentes*, or *residentes*) were perpetual tenants of their holdings. Farms passed from father to son for many generations, and we often find them described in deeds of sale, inheritance, and partition, by the tenant's own personal name.

The persistence of the same families on the same farms for generations and even centuries, and the survival of land divisions going back as far as Roman times, seem to suggest that, although waste land may have been cleared and drained in the Middle Ages, there can have been very little progress in agricultural technique. Land lost to cultivation during the decay of Rome, the barbarian invasions, and the depopulation of the countryside, was certainly brought back into use; but as far as we can judge (and our knowledge is admittedly slight), no advance was made beyond the agricultural practice described by Cato, Varro, and Columella.

The same crops were grown as before. The cereals still were wheat, spelt, barley, oats, millet, and also probably rye in the Alpine valleys. There is no evidence for the introduction of maize, frequently confused by historians with sorghum (*meliga, saggina*), which was in fact cultivated in many places. Of tree crops far the most widespread was the vine; and most of the leases for development, which survive in growing numbers from the ninth century on, were addressed to extending viticulture. Olive cultivation was much more restricted, but even so we find it practised during the Middle Ages in many parts of the Po valley and the Venetian plain. The mulberry was probably brought to Sicily by the Arabs. It then spread particularly to the coasts overlooking the Straits of Messina and later on, after the twelfth century, to the territory of Lucca and certain districts in northern Italy. But its progress was very slow, and down to the sixteenth century the Italian silk industry had to rely for its raw material on imports from the East.

The oldest Italian treatise on agriculture composed in the Middle Ages is that of the Bolognese jurist, Pietro dei Crescenzi. For the materials of his book, Crescenzi drew extensively upon the Roman agronomists; but he was also a shrewd and enthusiastic observer of the methods of cultivation used in the various districts of the Marche, Tuscany, Emilia, Piedmont, and Lombardy, which he had to visit in the course of his judicial activities. So for example, when discussing the vine, he describes the forms of cultivation current in Lombardy, Romagna, Modena, the March of Ancona, Pistoia, and Cortona. In one particular chapter, which is quite independent of his Latin authorities, he records the varieties of grape grown, not only in these regions, but also in the countryside of Padua, Pisa, Asti, and Ferrara; elsewhere, in a passage devoted to the pruning of vines, he turns for illustration to Asti, Crema, Milan, Bergamo, Verona, Bologna, Modena, and Forli. Among other crops he gives special attention to sorghum and hemp, plants which the ancients had disregarded almost entirely; and he pauses to investigate the various uses to which hemp may be put, indicating the places and methods of cultivation appropriate to the manufacture of rope, nets, sacking, and so on. We may conclude that, if a writer so attentive to actual conditions was normally content to reproduce the statements of Latin writers, he must have found what they had to say in general agreement with the practice of his time. This means that, despite the formation of a wealthy class of urban proprietors, Italian agriculture in the period of greatest communal prosperity was still mainly governed by the legacy of ancient Rome. Not before the mid sixteenth century do we begin to hear of isolated attempts to discard traditional principles for more rational and scientific methods.

b. Industry

Industries are nourished by markets and can only thrive in the neighbourhood of markets. It is not surprising therefore that during the age of the communes most industries were located in the towns.

The only exception to this, for obvious reasons, was the mining and smelting industry. Italy is notoriously poor in minerals, but this deficiency was much less acutely felt in the Middle Ages, when the great difficulty and cost of importing gold and silver from central and eastern Europe, and later on from Africa, encouraged exploitation of the most unrewarding resources. Thus the sands of certain Alpine streams were washed for gold, and silver was dug from mines in the Trentino and Cadore, Tuscany and Sardinia, which today have either been abandoned or are simply worked for lead and copper pyrites or iron. Gold-washing made little claims on labour or techniques. But mining was carried on during the communal period by fairly advanced methods, as we learn quite early from a Trentine codex of 1193. Galleries were made to follow the seams of ore; they were approached by inclined or vertical shafts, and had to be ventilated with special air-holes and drained with special pumps or tunnels. The ore itself was extracted with picks or by kindling large wood fires, which were set alight on non-working days to make the harder rocks more easy to dig. The miners worked a five-day week, each day being divided into two twelve-hour shifts. The work was complex, and the many operations in and round the mine not only employed a great variety of instruments, but also imposed a division of labour among the workmen themselves. Most of the workmen, particularly those with special skill in mining, were immigrants from Germany. Frequent migration, indeed, was part of the trade. It was a consequence of mining methods, by which each group of miners was only granted limited workings (*fosse*) to dig—according to the statutes never more than fifteen paces apart. As a result the seams were soon exhausted and the miners had to go in search of other concessions, often far away. The *fosse* were divided (in just the same way as merchant ships) into lots, 32 in all, which were shared in various proportions by the partners (*partiarii*) and represented a corresponding number of individual claims upon the total output of the group. But since the claims were heritable and alienable, they often passed in practice to persons wholly unconnected with mining, who lived for the most part in the towns and employed skilled men, unprovided with capital, to work their claims. So we find two distinct groups already formed in the thirteenth century: the partners (*partiarii*) and the workers (*laboratores*). As a general rule the entire mining concession was sub-let to a company of workers, who either took two-fifths of the metal extracted or kept it all to themselves and paid a rent to the various partners. In some places, however, particularly the Maremma, the partners chose one of the more expert workmen to serve as master, and he then hired other labourers by the week or the day and paid them with a share of the mineral.

Closely related to mining was the iron-smelting industry.

This was especially well developed in the valleys behind Bergamo and Brescia, where iron of the purest quality, highly valued in arms manufacture, was produced in small lots from numbers of tiny forges.

All the other industries of Italy were by this time located in the cities. They may be divided into two classes, of which the first, the most numerous, provided for the daily needs of the local town and country population, and the second, the more specialized, produced goods for a much wider market. Industries of the former kind were composed of artisans in the strict sense, working for a small number of customers, whose tastes and needs they understood and could easily assess in advance. Such men clearly avoided risks, but they also avoided profits. To them at least, and the petty merchants like them, it is proper to apply Sombart's definition of medieval business as a system organized for immediate consumption and not for profit. But side by side with the small local industries medieval Italy was quick to develop other, far larger enterprises, which often commanded vast international markets.

In the Middle Ages, unlike today, the leading place in industry was occupied, not by the so-called heavy industries, but by the manufacture of textiles, in particular woollens. The growth of woollen industries was obviously favoured wherever wool of suitable quality was in plentiful supply; but this was not an indispensable condition of development. The Mediterranean countries which grew the finest fleeces, the so-called *Garbo* wool and the wool of the Castilian tableland, were content for centuries to send their product abroad in the raw state. Even fifteenth-century England still exported more wool than cloth. On the other hand the major centres of the medieval woollen industry—Flanders, Brabant, and northern France, certain towns of southern France, Lombardy, Venetia, and Tuscany—did not derive their superiority from local flocks or pastures so much as from their trade, which enabled them to import choice wools easily, even from a distance.

It would certainly be absurd to claim that Italy ever attained supremacy in the manufacture of woollen cloth; this distinction belongs unquestionably to the countries of north-west Europe. But in the marketing of woollen cloth Italy was second to none.

In the large-scale export of northern cloth to the south and south-east, either from the centres of production or through the fairs of Champagne, Italian merchants were the most active and enterprising agents; and it was mainly due to them that northern draperies (the so-called "French" cloth) were able to reach the principal markets of the Mediterranean. From the eleventh century onwards, a growing number of "Lombard" merchants frequented the markets of France and the Low Countries, and this they did for the primary purpose of buying cloth. Indeed, the whole class of greater merchants in Italy built up their business and economic power on the local sale and re-export of foreign textiles. The Florentine Calimala guild is the most brilliant example of success in this lucrative trade, but the basis of mercantile activity was not substantially different in Lucca, Siena, Piacenza, Milan, or the other large communes of northern Italy.

In most of these communes, as we shall presently see, the cloth trade eventually stimulated the growth of a local woollen industry, also producing for export. But in certain places it acted rather as a check to local manufacture. At Genoa and Venice, at least, this was not simply due to pressure from the importers of foreign cloth. Not only the interests of a group were at stake, but the prosperity and even the survival of all maritime trade, especially trade with the Levant, where fine fabrics represented one of the few western products in great demand. We have clear proof of this in two Venetian tariffs of the thirteenth century, which mention cloth from only six Italian towns (Lucca, Florence, Milan, Como, Bergamo, Brescia), as against thirty different grades of woollen cloth, mostly of expensive quality, from twenty different towns of France, the Low Countries, and (in one case) England. It is obvious that any policy which might have favoured local industry at the expense of such invaluable imports would have impeded very seriously the flow of Oriental goods to Venice.

The position was different in the greater communes of the interior. In these towns the merchant class itself came to realize the advantages of combining home-produced with foreign cloth. The inland communes also commanded much more territory than either Genoa or Venice, from which a growing textile industry could draw supplies of raw material and labour. The actual extension of cloth production was the effect of various influences, both at home and abroad. At home, the rapid rise in urban population increased the demand for cheap inferior fabrics; while abroad, the decline of the fairs of Champagne, the repeated restrictions imposed on Italian trade, especially in France, and finally the improvement of shipping services, which made it easy to import high-grade wools from foreign countries like England, all encouraged Italian wool manufacturers to raise the quality of their products for purposes of export. Thus in Florence, according to Giovanni Villani, there were 300 workshops at the beginning of the fourteenth century producing yearly 100,000 pieces of cloth (i.e. one piece per shop per day), whereas thirty years later there were only 200 shops producing 70,000–80,000 pieces; but if the number of pieces had fallen, their value had also doubled, reaching a total of 1,200,000 gold florins or an average of 15 florins a piece, and this transformation, Villani explains, was mainly due to the recent introduction of English wool. As regards prices at least, Villani's figures are abundantly confirmed by the records of Venetian trade, which show that towards the middle of the fourteenth century the best Florentine cloth equalled or surpassed in value the most favoured fabrics of Flanders. It should be noted all the same that, while production flourished in the Florentine woollen industry, the twenty companies of the Calimala guild still found demand enough in the local market to justify the import of 10,000 pieces of foreign cloth, valued at 300,000 florins; and this was apart from other stocks, undefined but certainly large, which were destined for re-export.

Outside Florence the woollen industry also made rapid progress during the fourteenth century in the Lombard towns and certain towns of Venetia. Here too use was made of foreign wool, especially Spanish wool, imported by way of Pisa, Genoa, and Venice. And here too great strides were made in the technical organization and management of textile manufacture.

The organization of the woollen industry was controlled by the various technical processes, some fifteen in all, which were necessary for turning raw and dirty wool into finished cloth. Each of these processes was entrusted to special groups of workers who, apart from the spinners, were not allowed to sell the product of their industry, but only to pass it on to the men in charge of the next operation. This arrangement was enough by itself to create the need for entrepreneurs, who would buy raw material and pay for each successive stage of manufacture. But certain operations in particular demanded a complex organization and a substantial advance of capital; these were the finishing operations, applied to the woven cloth—cleansing, fulling, tentering, raising, shearing, dressing, and dyeing. In very small places, with a limited market for cloth, it is possible that all these processes were undertaken by one master craftsman, normally a weaver or dyer, and that customers were expected to pay part of the cost in advance. But in big towns, where production was largely for export and a fairly long period was bound to elapse between the purchase of the raw materials and the sale of the finished goods, the whole organization was inevitably dependent on capitalist entrepreneurs, who could pay all or most of the cost in advance, and also market the cloth. These men, as we have said, might be actual workers in the industry, such as weavers or dyers; but mostly they were merchants, the so-called drapers or *lanaiuoli* (wool manufacturers), who apart from selling cloth retail also engaged in the export trade. Technically they were still artisans, but in practice they performed the functions of the merchant entrepreneurs, who often disposed of insufficient resources and were obliged to enter into partnership with other capitalists. At the other extreme stood the workers employed in the preliminary operations of cloth manufacture, who were wage-labourers, usually hired by the day.

Of the metal industries the only one about which we have any information (apart from what is contained in guild regulations) is the arms industry, which reached the peak of perfection and production in fourteenth-century Milan. The industry was favoured by the command of excellent raw material from the ironworks of the Alpine valleys and Lombardy, and was also greatly stimulated by the rapid increase in demand for weapons which accompanied the replacement of urban militias by mercenary troops after the middle of the thirteenth century. About that time, according to Bonvesin della Ripa, Milan alone possessed over one hundred workshops producing body armour, apart from numerous other shops which turned out weapons of every kind. Even today, in the centre of the city, there is an "Armourer St.", "Swordsmith St.", and "Spurrier St." In the later fourteenth century, during the most critical period of the War of Chioggia, one of the most eminent citizens of Venice was sent on an urgent mission to Milan to buy up arms, and in very little time he was supplied with 1,230 corselets, 1,492 helmets, and 180,000 crossbow bolts, costing in all 7,200 gold ducats. This Milanese arms industry, which acquired an international reputation by manufacturing corselets of the finest steel mail, owed its excellence to the personal skill of the craftsmen. For this reason production was never centralized but was carried on by individual masters in their own shops, with the help of a few companions and apprentices. Generally they worked on their own account and dealt directly with their clients.

A more distinctly capitalist structure is evident, from the thirteenth century on, in the shipbuilding industry, at least at Genoa and Venice. The *Annals* of the chronicler Caffaro show that, from quite an early date, private and public enterprise collaborated in the building of galleys at Genoa, and that the government often made use of merchant shipping. Shipbuilding was financed in the case of private vessels by the shipowners themselves, and was organized on a basis of contracts and subcontracts, whereby the work was first entrusted to a master shipwright, who then shared it out among various specialized craftsmen employing wage-labour. At Venice, shipbuilding was carried on in two forms, public and private. The public industry was located in the famous Arsenal, while private shipbuilding was dispersed in a large number of smaller shipyards or *squeri*, at Venice itself, Chioggia, and on various islands of the estuary. As a rule the state looked after the navy, and private industry took care of the merchant marine; but quite often private shipyards also were commissioned to build galleys and other warships. The workers in the Arsenal, even skilled workers qualified as masters, were all wage-labourers. Private shipbuilding, by contrast, retained more the forms of an artisan organization, to the extent at least that every process of construction was assigned to separate master craftsmen, each of whom was assisted by a small group of workers and apprentices and was inscribed as a member of the guild of caulkers (*calafati*) or carpenters (*marangoni*). But essentially most of these masters, like most of the masters of the Arsenal, were nothing more than trained workmen, drawing a daily or weekly wage and their keep from an entrepreneur. Only a very small number formed a kind of aristocracy apart, the so-called *protomaestri*, who took contracts for particular jobs of construction or repair and directed the work of groups of masters. At Venice, as at Genoa, the actual risks and costs of construction were covered by the shipowners. Not even the owners of the shipyards, the *squeraroli*, normally did more than make occasional repairs or build a few light craft for inland traffic; their activity was generally limited to letting out sections of their yard for shipowners to build in.

Quite different from this, and entirely individualistic in character, were the art industries which started to develop in various Italian cities during the fourteenth century. These industries, however, only attained their fullest splendour after the fifteenth century, and we must therefore postpone all treatment of them until a later chapter.

c. Commerce

i. The range of Italian commerce. If industry made great advances in the communal age, and even agriculture, which is slow to change, recovered the ground once lost during the decline of Rome and the barbarian invasions, it was commerce more than anything that raised Italy to undisputed supremacy in the economy of the medieval world. Indeed, it was to satisfy the needs of international commerce that technology and legal institutions were improved and business organization put upon a rational basis, that the spirit of initiative and enterprise was developed to the highest degree, and a new social type, the modern entrepreneur, was brought into being. There were no boundaries for the merchants of medieval Italy; their activities traversed the entire known world and penetrated into unfamiliar regions with which westerners had had no direct contact before the thirteenth century. The best-known commercial manual of the time, the *Pratica della mercatura*, written in the first half of the fourteenth century by Francesco Pegolotti, a representative of the great Bardi company of Florence, passes in review an astonishing number of trading centres in the Old

World, extending far beyond the limits of the ancient Roman Empire. Not only the Mediterranean and the Black Sea towns find a place in this treatise, but also many countries further east: Armenia and Persia, the Caspian coastlands, Turkestan, Mongolia, and China. Clearly the voyages undertaken by the Polo family had not been isolated ventures, the disregarded exploits of ardent pioneers; other merchants from other towns had followed in their footsteps, enticed by the prospect of profitable business. Such journeys may not have been frequent, for the distances involved were enormous, and Pegolotti himself calculates that 250 days were needed to get from Caffa (Feodosia) in the Crimea to Peking; but relations with the East were evidently close enough to justify his giving detailed information about the coinage and paper money, the weights and measures, and the commercial practices of these remote places.

In Africa, Italian merchants travelled no further south than Cairo and the Atlantic coast of Morocco. But in the fifteenth century a number of enterprising navigators, Venetians and still more Genoese, were enlisted by the Portuguese court in voyages of discovery southward from Morocco. In the Iberian peninsula the Italians frequented the Mediterranean ports of the Balearics, Barcelona, Valencia, and Almeria, and the Atlantic ports of Lisbon and Cadiz; after the middle of the thirteenth century they also began to invade the great commercial centre of Seville. In France and the Low Countries Italians travelled everywhere; in England they were mostly to be met with in London and Southampton.

Apart from the cities which Pegolotti lists, we have clear and abundant evidence of Italians trading in many other towns which he ignores, possibly because the Florentines did not go there. If we add these to the reckoning, then we must include in the range of Italian commerce all the countries of central Europe, in particular the Rhineland and the upper and middle Danube, from which Italian merchants passed to Poland and the Baltic.

ii. Transport and communications. This enormous expansion in the range of commerce was not matched by any comparable improvement in the means of transport and communication. Considerable progress was made, to be sure, in the building of roads and canals, but this was confined to the territory of particular communes or, later on, to particular regions, mainly in Tuscany and the Po valley. Across the Apennines and Alps the roads were such that goods could only be carried on the backs of men or pack-animals or at best on tiny carts. In the lowlands a great deal of traffic moved by waterway. Thus in Tuscany the Arno was used for navigation, though this was possible only at certain times of the year and along the stretch between Signa and Pisa; from Pisa to Porto Pisano and from the Arno to the Serchio, numerous canals had to be cut for the convenience of traffic between Lucca, Pisa, and the sea. River navigation had far greater importance in the valley of the Po, especially on the lower reaches between Piacenza and the coast. The Venetian lagoon was connected by canal with the Adige and the Po. In 1220, when the Mantuans were threatening to divert all traffic on the Po to their city, the communes of Cremona and Reggio combined to defeat the design by building a grand navigation canal some forty miles long, which after leaving the Po at Guastalla, where the river turns north, re-entered it at the mouth of the Panaro. Even towns which did not lie along the Po, in particular Milan, Bergano, Lodi, Brescia, Parma, Reggio, Modena, and Bologna, were all connected with it by rivers or canals and all maintained their tiny ports.

Conditions of travel were far worse in those parts of Italy which possessed no great communes or wealthy business class. The journey from Florence to Naples, which merchants sometimes managed to complete in eleven or twelve days by riding from morning to night and travelling via Terni, Aquila, Sulmona, and Teano, bristled with difficulties and dangers. The only way across the Abruzzi was by rough country track, and the borders of Campania were infested with brigands. The shortest route from Rome to Naples, the road through Terracina, had such an evil reputation that only troops and public officials dared to use it, while all trade went round by sea. Beyond Naples, the only major highway was the ancient road leading from Campania to Foggia and Manfredonia (Siponto): this could carry small carts and was used extensively by merchants.

Even greater difficulties had to be faced by Italians travelling overland to the fairs of Champagne, to Paris, and to Flanders.

Politics often played a part, and so forbidding were the hazards that merchants commonly preferred to go by sea to the ports of Provence and then proceed by way of the Rhône and Saône to their northern destinations. Even so, the shorter Alpine route was never entirely neglected, in spite of serious obstacles. There were numerous passes over the Alps, from the Little St. Bernard in the west to the Pontebba in the east, but the tracks were rough and steep and the carriage of all goods had to be entrusted to local people, since every tiny Alpine commune held a monopoly of transport through its territory. These privileges, which made it necessary to change the carriers (*vetturali*) at every stage, only served to make the journey longer. Six days were needed to make the relatively short crossing from Chiavenna to Chur.

But if transport was slow, postal services by land were comparatively quick. During the communal period, from about 1300 onward, increasing use was made of couriers by all kinds of institutions: monasteries and universities, the governments of the greater communes, and most of all the merchant guilds. Couriers usually travelled on horseback, riding either the whole journey or between established stages, where post-horses were kept. By such means, with a little luck, the entire route from Venice to Bruges could be covered in seven or eight days.

Incomparably cheaper and safer than movement overland was movement by river. In Italy, however, river-transport was only practicable in certain regions and over relatively short distances. And so throughout the Middle Ages much the most active highway of communication was the sea.

Sea transport also had its perils, some of them natural, some contrived by men. Thus the danger of shipwreck, to which the small craft of the time were frequently exposed, was aggravated by the survival of the right of wreck (*jus naufragii*), by which lords and communes were permitted to seize all goods thrown up on the shores of their territory. But the greatest menace to merchant shipping was piracy, which some maritime communities made their principal occupation. Even when the use of the compass facilitated long-distance navigation in the open sea, the lack of security, especially in waters far from home, maintained the habit of travelling in convoy with naval escort.

All these dangers explain the custom of dividing the ownership of vessels among several partners, who shared the risks in proportion to their holdings. Similar reasons lay behind the widespread popularity of the sea loan, which not only increased the amount of money invested in one enterprise, but also extended the risks of navigation to a capitalist who owned no part of the ship. Frequent recourse to loans of this kind, it is plausibly suggested, eventually encouraged the development of marine insurance, which after the early years of the fourteenth century we begin to find in fairly general use.

In spite of the dangers, however, sea communication was still much the most preferred method of travel, even for journeys that could be made by land, because it offered the means of transporting heavy, bulky, and inexpensive goods. It is true that even merchant ships were of very small tonnage in the Middle Ages, though after the thirteenth century they tended to increase in size, especially those which braved the Atlantic or were destined for the distant Black Sea. According to the maritime laws of Venice, compiled in the first half of the thirteenth century, merchant ships varied in capacity from 200 to 1,000 *libbre grosse*, or from 94 to 470 tons. But in the centuries following, the galleys and other vessels (*cocche*), which plied the three routes to Flanders, Syria, and Constantinople (with the Black Sea), were conspicuously larger: by the early fifteenth century the Flanders boats exceeded 750 tons, while the others ranged from 600 to 800 tons.

iii. The volume of trade. If we were lucky enough to possess trade statistics relating to the ports of Genoa and Venice during the period of their greatest prosperity and placed them beside similar figures of our own day from New York, London, Antwerp, Rotterdam, or Hamburg, we should be immediately struck by the comparative insignificance of medieval trade. Such a comparison, however, even if it were possible, would not provide decisive proof that commerce was negligible in the communal age, because modern statistics are enormously distended by the trade in such extremely cheap and bulky goods as mineral oils and coal, iron ore, phosphates, cement materials, and so on, all of which were quite unknown in the Middle Ages. At that time, admittedly, the demand for foreign wares was very small in volume, because the population was much less dense than now and the lower orders of society, both in the country and to a great extent also in the town, had no share in it whatever. This is well shown by the simple case of the woollen industry, which spread to many small towns, and even to *castelli*, precisely in order to supply the needs of humble people, who had to be content with second-rate cloth woven from local wool. The top-grade wools, imported from Morocco, Spain, and England, were reserved for upper-class needs.

All the same, the flourishing state of the Italian towns between the thirteenth century and the first half of the six-teenth was not built exclusively on trade in high-quality merchandise; in practice much the greater part of the goods which Italians shipped by sea consisted not of gold or silver or slaves, or the precious products of the East, but of wool, cotton, silk, salt, wheat, sugar, wine, timber, iron, copper, dye-stuffs, and alum. Sombart has challenged Villani's well-known figures for Florentine industry on the grounds that a yearly production of 100,000 pieces of cloth is hardly compatible with an import of only 4,000 sacks of English wool, which would yield at most 12,000 pieces. But he overlooked the fact that not only English wool was used in the production of the best Florentine fabrics, but also *Garbo* wool, Spanish wool, and wool from the Apennines and other parts of Italy, which may all have been imported in far larger quantity.

iv. Markets and fairs. Small merchants and great merchants. In the Italian towns of the Middle Ages which played most part in international trade, we find two types of merchants living side by side, differing profoundly in their form of activity, manner of life, and business outlook. There was first of all the small merchant, the shopkeeper, who as an economic figure was hardly distinguishable from the artisan. This man spent the day behind his shop-counter, selling miscellaneous wares to a small and barely changing group of customers, and exercised his trade subject to regulation and inspection by his guild and by the government officials charged with control of the market. He earned enough to support his family, but could rarely hope to widen the range of his affairs or multiply his profits.

Much of the business done by small traders of this kind was

transacted in daily and weekly markets where people from the country round about exchanged their produce for the manufactures of urban craftsmen. The infrequent mention of annual fairs in both documents and chronicles is probably due to the fact that in the greater commercial cities trade in all commodities, whether local or foreign, went on all through the year. The only exceptions, outside the March of Ancona, the Abruzzi, Apulia, and a few other southern districts, were certain towns in the valleys of the Po and Adige (Piacenza, Bologna, Ferrara, Trent, Bolzano) which, mainly for geographical reasons, were the meeting-place of important fairs throughout the Middle Ages and beyond. Best known are the fairs of Ferrara, a town situated at the intersection of the Po and the highways from Romagna, Tuscany, Mantua, and Verona. They were held twice a year, at Easter and Martinmas, and were frequented by merchants from Bologna, Mantua, Milan, and other Lombard towns, as well as by Tuscans and occasional foreigners, who were attracted by the trade in cloth, skins, metalwork, and other goods.

With the Italian fairs, limited though their function may have been, we begin to leave the small world of local trade for the wider horizons of inter-regional and international trade on the grand scale. This was the exclusive concern of the great merchants, who in the Italian towns of the Middle Ages formed a class entirely separate from the petty shopkeepers. In places where commerce was most intense and throve in combination with industry, we do not find a single comprehensive merchant guild but rather a number of different corporations, each representing a particular branch of trade and sometimes associated with a corresponding branch of industry. Instead of the merchant guild there existed a board of magistrates, a public commission called the *Mercanzia*. At Genoa and Venice, where the commune itself formed the corporation of the commercial aristocracy, the great merchants did not feel any need to combine in professional guilds, but preferred to use the guild organization, especially in Venice, as a means of control and domination over the much more numerous class of artisans. The very fact that there were guilds of haberdashers, grocers, and second-hand dealers (*rivenduglioli*), and none at all of money-changers and bankers, cloth merchants and shipowners, is enough to show

how radical and universally acknowledged was the difference between the shopkeeper, who was treated much like an artisan, and the merchant, in the loftier sense of the word, who invested his time and capital in international trade and enjoyed full political rights. Even when the greater merchants—like those of the Calimala guild at Florence—combined big business with shopkeeping, their mode of training and *curriculum vitae*, which varied very little from one large commercial town to another, still marked them off emphatically from the petty local tradesmen. After taking a course in grammar and arithmetic (including commercial arithmetic), they began their career at a very early age with a number of protracted journeys over land and sea. Often they spent long periods in foreign countries, representing the family business or the firm in which members of their family were the leading partners, and transacting other affairs on behalf of relatives and friends. A few even finished up their wanderings from one great town to another by settling permanently abroad. But most of them came home after reaching middle age, though not in order to retire; on the contrary, they now took charge of operations at the centre, maintaining close contact with the foreign agencies and branches of their business, even when invested with high offices of state.

As for the quantity of business done, though it may be true that merchants were often ready to devote unlimited time and patience to obtaining a few pieces of cloth, or write numerous letters and engage in prolonged litigation for the sake of a few dozen ducats, there is still plenty of evidence of larger transactions, which even in our own day would be judged important. When the books of the Bardi company were balanced on 1 July 1318, they registered a total turnover of 873,638 gold florins. Even when the figures for individual transactions seem pitifully small, it must always be remembered that most great merchants dealt in a wide variety of goods. To take just one example: the merchandise, in store or still at sea, which was sold up by the executors of the Venetian, Pietro Soranzo, on his death in the second half of the fourteenth century consisted of pepper, valued at 3,000 ducats, nutmegs, cloves, tin, lead, and iron, valued at much the same amount, gold from Russia worth 1,478 ducats, raw silk worth 3,810 ducats, and Russian skins worth 1,900 ducats, together with a quantity of Syrian and Cypriot sugar,

wax, honey, and pearls, of which the value, though not precisely
stated, was certainly high. About the same period the brothers
Cornaro entered into partnership with a certain Vito Lion,
gentleman of Verona, to carry on trade with Cyprus; their
joint capital amounted to 83,273 ducats and their imports for
a single year were worth 67,000 ducats.

Beyond a doubt the pace of medieval business was very slow.
Thus, it took four months, on an average, to transport a bale of
cloth from Flanders to Florence. But before the age of steam
and the telegraph, the speed of communications was never much
increased, yet this did not prevent the Fuggers and other business houses from amassing gigantic fortunes in the sixteenth
century. To big firms, with branches in all the main markets of
the world and a substantial turnover of business in every one,
the slow rate of each transaction scarcely mattered; and it
certainly did not stop them from making very large total profits,
even though the average return from commercial investments
was relatively small (according to Sapori between 10 and 15
per cent). At the time of his death, early in the fourteenth
century, the total patrimony of Bartolo di Jacopo Bardi
amounted to no more than 17,240 florins in movable goods
and 8,400 florins in landed property. Less than forty years
later his sons had increased the family fortune to 129,142 florins,
and this they accomplished entirely by trade and banking.

But the magnitude and modernity, so to speak, of large-scale
Italian commerce during the thirteenth and still more the fourteenth centuries is most clearly displayed in the complex and
systematic organization of business houses. In the space of
thirty-six years, between 1310 and 1345, the Bardi company
employed altogether 346 agents (*fattori*). Since each agent remained in the service of the firm for an average of eleven to
twelve years, it follows that every year the company must have
had between 100 and 120 employees on its books. The members
of this staff received various rates of pay, ranging from 5 to 7
gold florins per annum for apprentices, to 200 florins for branch-
managers in Flanders and England, and 300 florins for directors
in charge of accounts at the centre. All these agents were distributed over 25 different branches: 12 in Italy, 4 in the Levant,
and 9 in France, the Low Countries, England, Spain, and
Tunis.

With firms of this complexity and size to manage, Italian merchants were bound to develop entirely new methods of organization, administration, and accounting; and it was thanks to them if rapid progress in the sciences of reckoning and book-keeping, commercial technique and law, made Italy the business school of Europe during the fourteenth and fifteenth centuries.

v. The forms of investment in international trade. It appears, then, that the great merchant of medieval Italy was preeminently a man of enterprise and resource, generously endowed with the spirit of initiative and organization, who was ready to engage in all kinds of affairs: foreign and domestic trade, both whole-sale and retail, dealings in cloth or raw wool, grain, spices, salt, or metals, the financing of industry and the business of exchange, loans to private citizens and princes, communes, or despots, and the farming of customs and taxes. But the personal capital with which the merchant first ventured on these various activities was generally insufficient; gradually therefore, as the scope of his business widened, he sought among his relatives and friends, or among other merchants at home and abroad, men who were prepared to entrust him with their capital for some particular enterprise, or join with him as partners in all his undertakings for a stated length of time. The forms of capital investment and partnership varied. In particular, those employed in maritime trade differed from those developed in trade by land.

The two forms of contract most generally favoured in the maritime towns between the twelfth and the fourteenth centuries were the sea loan and the *commenda*, or what was called in Venice the *colleganza*. The sea loan was an advance of money by a capitalist to a merchant or ship's captain at the start of a trading voyage; the money travelled at the lender's risk, and was repaid with interest (generally very high interest) on arrival at the port of destination or return to the port of embarkation. In many, perhaps the majority of cases, a clause was inserted requiring restitution in a different coinage from that of the original payment, which converted the loan into a contract of exchange (*a cambio marittimo*). Widespread though it was, the sea loan was much less common a form of investment in over-seas trade than the *commenda*, a type of contract admirably designed for granting people in all walks of life a chance to share in the expected profits of maritime commerce, without the dangers and discomforts of a voyage by sea. *Commenda* contracts were of two kinds, bilateral and unilateral, and these survive in roughly equal numbers in the records. In the case of the bilateral *commenda* (which the Genoese called a *societas*), the partner who stayed at home (the *stans*) contributed two-thirds of the capital, while the seafaring merchant who managed the venture (the *procertans* or *tractator*) contributed only a third. By the unilateral *commenda*, or *commenda* proper, the *stans* provided all the capital and reserved three-fourths of the profits. In practice, however, both types of agreement were probably unilateral in character, and the fiction of bilateral investment may have been introduced into the contract to justify the division of the risks, which were not assumed entirely by the lender, as in the sea loan, but were shared in the proportion of two-thirds and one-third by the *stans* and the *procertans*. The relationship of merchant and capitalist was essentially one between debtor and creditor, with the simple but significant difference that the merchant was bound not only to repay the borrowed money with all agreed interest, but also to render account of the business transacted with the money or merchandise entrusted to him "in commenda", and justify any failure to repay the full sum invested. The German historian Sombart, determined at all costs to minimize the volume of traffic in the communal age, makes fun of the merchants who set off on "great" trading enterprises with a mere hundred Genoese pounds commended to them; but he overlooks the numerous surviving *commenda* contracts for much larger sums, and forgets that the same merchant would normally receive a dozen or several dozen commissions of the kind at one time. Both at Genoa and at Venice the *commenda* became the most favoured and frequent type of investment during the thirteenth century. To quote one example: at the time of his death in 1268, the Venetian doge Ranieri Zeno still had pending 132 contracts of *colleganza*, representing 22,935 *lire* out of a total personal estate of 38,848 *lire*. Not only this; the same doge accompanied the legacies granted in his will to relatives and religious, churches and monasteries, with a recommendation, and often a stipulation, that the same form of investment should continue to be used. This attitude was not peculiar to the Venetians, but was equally common among the merchants of Pisa, Genoa, Marseilles, and Barcelona.

Profoundly different from these seafaring partnerships were the forms of commercial partnership which prevailed in the towns of the interior and which began to spread, after the thirteenth century, to the coastal cities as well. The capital for a commercial company was subscribed, in varying proportions, by a whole group of people, most of whom belonged to one family, so that companies were generally known by a family name. Unlike the seafaring partnerships, which were formed for the duration of only one trading venture and then dissolved, commercial companies were established to carry on business of many different kinds during a specified length of time. At the end of the period the firm was dissolved, but in normal circumstances a new company was immediately formed, either with the same partners as before or with some fresh members added. Liability for debts was the collective responsibility of all the partners, and profits were divided, on liquidation, in proportion to each partner's initial investment.

vi. Accounting. The merchants of medieval Italy were not obliged by law to keep accounts, but as business expanded in range and complexity, they found it increasingly convenient to do so; and once partnerships became the rule in the larger commercial enterprises, systematic bookkeeping was unavoidable. At first, no doubt, the main object in bookkeeping was simply to preserve a record of transactions which had not been promptly settled in cash; later on, however, these rough memoranda were supplemented by a complete, co-ordinated set of books, which made it possible to trace every stage of the firm's business. The practice now began of keeping a day-book, recording each day's operations, and a ledger (*libro mastro*), in which every person dealing regularly with the firm was entered, with a separate account, on a separate page, under his own name, with the debit column (*dare*) on the left side and the credit column (*avere*) on the right. At the same time we begin to encounter the system of double-entry bookkeeping, in which every transaction is entered twice in the same register, once on the debit side and once on the credit side; it was possible to give this double character to each transaction by representing things as well as persons as creditors and debtors. The invention of the double-entry system was long attributed to Luca Paciolo of Borgo San Sepolcro, who in his *Summa de Arithmetica*, published at Venice in 1494, described this method of accounting in great detail. The truth is, however, that the learned friar invented nothing; all he did, as he says himself, was give an accurate exposition of accounting methods which had long been used in the business houses of Venice (whence the name *scrittura alla Veneziana*), Florence, Genoa, and Milan.

4. FINANCE, MONEY, AND CREDIT IN THE AGE OF THE COMMUNES

a. Finance

As early as the eleventh century the Italian towns had ceased to perform their ancient function as mere fiscal organs of the state, and begun to advance rapidly towards effective financial autonomy. Full autonomy they may never have achieved, but fiscal independence became virtually unlimited in the communes of Lombardy and Tuscany. In the States of the Church the financial independence of the towns was restricted by papal sovereignty, while in the south of Italy it was reduced to insignificance by the Norman and Hohenstaufen monarchy, which stubbornly opposed all forms of local privilege and self-government. In the great communes of upper Italy, where the pulse of economic life beat more vigorously and urban government became all but sovereign after the fall of the Hohenstaufen, a fiscal system developed which, although influenced by late Roman and Germanic institutions, was essentially new both in form and complexity.

In all medieval towns, great and small, we find a common disparity between regular and irregular income and expenditure. Thus the earliest surviving Venetian "budget" (*Regolazione*) of 1262 assigns to current expenditure the modest sum of 3,000 *lire a piccoli* per month, and this was meant to cover all costs of administration, which individual departments were unable to meet from their own particular revenue. All other income directly reaching the government was earmarked to pay the six-monthly 5 per cent interest on the public debt and the standing expenses of the armed forces and public works; any surplus was to be set aside for the amortization of debts. Despite its obvious inadequacy, the sum of 3,000 *lire* was only doubled in 1349.

In the early days of the communes, when wars were brief and local armies consisted of unpaid conscript militias, war expenditure was insignificant. But after the mid thirteenth century, when wars increased in scope and duration and urban militias were gradually supplanted by mercenary troops, expenses knew no bounds. The war with the Pope in 1375–8 cost Florence the substantial sum of 2,500,000 gold florins; and this enormous charge was subsequently trebled by the three wars with the Visconti. At Venice, during the War of Chioggia (1378–81), not only were taxes sharply increased and large sums raised by voluntary contributions, but forced loans also were levied to a total amount of over 5,000,000 gold ducats.

Most mercenary companies were doubtless hired for the duration of a war and then discharged; but the greater communes, and even more the despots, who had to provide for internal security, also maintained a peace-time force of mercenaries, a bodyguard of troops, which eventually came to form the nucleus of a standing army. Another charge on urban revenues, though nothing like so heavy, was the professional bureaucracy, which developed during this period and encroached increasingly upon the functions of the older honorary magistracies. On all sides, therefore, the great cities of Renaissance Italy were faced with financial demands quite unknown to the monarchies of the early Middle Ages; and they were forced to create a system of regular and supplementary revenues which, however casual and improvised in character, really laid the foundations of modern state finance.

In the finances of the Italian communes income from land did not occupy the dominant place it had formerly held in the finances of the Italian Crown and the great feudal lordships. At the time of their formation, most communes were able to dispose of pastures and woods, over which the citizens exercised rights of common use; but they owned no cultivated land which might have yielded income of some importance. Later on, as a result of factious conflict and the conquest of neighbouring towns, both of which involved the expropriation of recalcitrant urban families, some of the larger communes did come into possession of very extensive estates; but the income arising was still quite inadequate to cover their rapidly mounting expenditure. More substantial was the income from urban property, especially the rent from booths, lots, and warehouses in and round the market-place. But even this was small compared with the yield of indirect taxes, levied on food and other prime necessities, on imports and exports, and on business transactions. Taxes of this kind, indeed, were the most productive source of what we may call ordinary revenue, although they varied sharply in time of war.

Direct taxes, by contrast, usually took the form of extraordinary levies, down to the fifteenth century. In the towns which had once been part of the Lombard and Carolingian kingdom, direct taxes retained the double character, inherited from the late Roman Empire, of personal taxes imposed by "hearths" (*fuochi*, *fumantes*) and property taxes imposed by valuation (*per libram*). In the case of personal taxes the only preliminary measure required was a census of all the households subject to contribution, each of which, as need arose, was called upon to pay a certain number of pence or sometimes a few shillings. Taxes *per libram*, on the other hand, were levied on the basis of an *estimo* or assessment of each man's total wealth in land and movables, calculated upon the taxpayer's own declaration, checked and if necessary revised by a commission of *allibratores* or *aestimatores*.

However, the method of raising revenues for extraordinary occasions, which was most generally adopted in the cities of Genoa, Florence, and Venice, was not taxation at all, but government borrowing. To begin with all public loans were voluntary loans, bearing variable rates of interest according to market conditions. They were secured upon particular revenues or classes of revenue, which were sometimes transferred to the lenders themselves and sometimes retained by the state, but only on the strict understanding that the interest was regularly paid and the principal refunded whenever possible. At Genoa, where this system developed further and lasted longer than anywhere else, loans to the commune were divided into groups, called *compere* ("purchases"), corresponding to the items of revenue assigned for their repayment. In order to remedy the disorder which inevitably accompanied such methods of public finance, the government tried to consolidate the public debt, but at first its success was compromised by the need to raise new loans to meet the cost of fresh wars and other unforeseen emergencies; and not until 1405 was the Genoese debt finally consolidated, with the establishment of the Casa di S. Giorgio, which we shall have occasion to consider later on.

At Florence and Venice, down to about 1200, the public debt hardly differed in form from that of Genoa. In these towns also voluntary loans were the rule. But during the thirteenth century the system of forced loans came to prevail. At Florence the system soon bulked large in public finance, especially in the years after 1315, when the *estimo* was suppressed outright and direct taxation was abandoned in favour of compulsory loans, which were interest-bearing and redeemable. By a reform of 1347 the various loans, which up to then had formed a floating debt, subject to various rates of interest and secured upon different items of the revenue, were consolidated into a funded debt, which yielded a fixed interest of 5 per cent and was freely negotiable. At Venice forced loans are first clearly attested in 1207, and they were organized into a permanent debt, at 5 per cent fixed interest, in 1262. In this city compulsory loans not only supplanted all direct taxation (which was only briefly revived during the War of Chioggia) but also became the exclusive form of public borrowing; voluntary loans were still raised in times of urgent need, but they were treated as a floating debt, to be extinguished with the proceeds of the next compulsory loan. Venetian loans were not imposed for a predetermined amount, but were levied by charging each taxpayer with a proportion of his *estimo* above a minimum originally fixed at 100 *lire* and subsequently raised to 300 *lire*. Down to 1363 the public debt remained redeemable, though not in the sense that repayment was promised within a stated time or over a stated period, but in the sense that the government, in years of prosperity and peace, set aside substantial sums (up to 22,500 *lire a grossi* per month) for discharge of the principal. In 1363, however, this practice was abandoned for the alternative system of using surplus revenue to buy up shares of the debt at market-prices. Government stocks were freely negotiable and varied continuously in market-price. Down to 1378 prices fluctuated between fairly narrow limits, ranging from 60 to 102 per cent of face-value; but in the third year of the War of Chioggia they dropped to 18 per cent. Prior to this the contributors to government loans, who numbered little over 2,000 out of a total population approaching 100,000, can scarcely have considered their payments oppressive. Government securities yielded a sure if limited interest and they could be sold on the market at any time without serious loss. Except during the four years 1350–3, when loans were levied up to a total of 40 per cent of taxable wealth, the burden imposed was certainly never severe, if only because the assessments on which loans were based were gravely inadequate. If the estimate of landed properties, which were valued at ten times the rental, probably did not fall far below market values, it is certain that the estimate of movables was grossly insufficient, because the figures returned by the taxpayers were always trifling and no means existed of checking their declarations. It was this sharp disparity between estimated and actual wealth that made it possible to raise a 40 per cent levy in 1350–3 without causing an upheaval in economic life. But the system of forced loans was carried to intolerable extremes during the War of Chioggia, when the Venetians were made to contribute sums exceeding their taxable estate, and the payment of interest was altogether suspended, causing government shares to fall abruptly in price. Even the richest taxpayers suffered by this absurd and iniquitous policy, for they were forced to purchase each new issue of war loan at face-value and then re-sell it at a fourth or a fifth of the purchase price to *nouveaux riches*, many of whom were not yet assessed to taxation at all. In these conditions a resumption of direct taxes became inevitable. A start was made as early as 1378, when a levy was introduced to pay the cost of equipping war-galleys, and a system of *impositiones* was adopted in the form of a deduction from official salaries, from the interest due on government securities, and from the rents owed for houses and other property. These *impositiones* should have been refunded at the end of the war, but in practice they were either forcibly converted into government stocks or left unpaid altogether. The return to direct taxation proceeded gradually down to the year

1463, when, as we shall see, a new permanent income tax (*decima*) was finally established.

b. Money, prices and wages

Among the regalian rights most jealously guarded by the royal and imperial fisc was the privilege of coining money. The right of coinage was valued not merely as a source of revenue, but also as a symbol of sovereignty, and for this reason was only granted to certain of the greater communes, after prolonged evasion and resistance.

As already noted, the only money generally coined in Italian mints, down to the fourteenth century, was the silver penny (*denaro*), which varied in alloy and weight from one mint to another and from one period to another, with a constant and uniform tendency to debasement. Without going back to the original penny of Charlemagne, which was meant to contain 1·7 grams of silver, it is enough to point out that as late as the second half of the twelfth century the penny of Lucca and Pisa, which was one of the most esteemed, still preserved a silver content of 0·6 gram, whereas fifty years later this had dropped to 0·25 gram. The frequent variation and continuous deterioration of the coinage were partly caused by the technical difficulty of meeting an increasing demand for money from an inelastic supply of silver. But the principal cause was the fiscal policy of the greater urban communes and princes, who regarded debasement of the coinage as a simple means of raising revenue without imposing any apparent charge upon their subjects. They found support for this convenient system in the so-called Nominalist doctrine, according to which the value of money was fixed by the will of the sovereign (*valor impositus*), as opposed to the Realist doctrine, according to which the value of money was limited by the value of the metal it contained (*bonitas intrinseca*). It should be added that, in those towns which developed large industries, persistent debasement of the smaller fractional coinage may have been influenced by the economic purpose of keeping down wages (which were paid in petty coin), thereby lowering costs of production in the interest of exports.

Meantime, however, as overseas trade expanded from the

twelfth century on, the communes most actively engaged in international commerce were faced with the problem of finding suitable media of exchange. They solved this in part by using foreign gold coin, mainly Byzantine, but also Arab coin. Another device they adopted was that of fixing prices, not in terms of the pound-tale of debased and unstable pennies (*libra denariorum*), but in terms of the pound-weight of pure silver (*libra argenti ponderati*), for which the commonest weight in use was the "Mark of Cologne", standardized at 233·8 grams. This practice persisted (or was possibly revived) as late as the sixteenth century, but its inconvenience was obvious; and so, about 1200, we find the Italian communes, as well as certain other states which played an active part in long-distance trade, proceeding to issue silver coins of a purity and stability which would make them generally acceptable in markets everywhere. The first town to do this, apparently, was Venice, which on the eve of the Fourth Crusade, when Enrico Dandolo was doge, began to strike *denari grossi* (large pennies or "groats"), with a silver content of 96·5 per cent and a total weight of 2·18 grams. The old penny, which soon acquired the name of the "small" penny (*piccolo*), stood to the new penny in the relation of 1 : 26·9. The result was that two different pounds (*lire*) now existed side by side, each subdivided into 20 shillings of 12 pence apiece, but widely divergent in value; the pound of large pence corresponded to 504·72 grams of pure silver, but the pound of small pence to only 19·33 grams. The *grosso* was destined to serve the needs of large-scale commerce and credit, while the *piccolo* was used in the local trade of town and countryside and in the payment of wages.

For the space of sixty years the relation of *grosso* and *piccolo* did not vary. Then complications began to arise. While the *grosso* remained unaltered, at Venice, for nearly 200 years (till 1379), the *piccolo* deteriorated rapidly. As early as 1265 the legal rate of exchange with the *grosso* had fallen to 27; in 1269 it stood at 28, and in 1282 at 32. This decline of the *piccolo*, which was the commonest coin in local use, was never successfully arrested, and its relation with the *grosso* fluctuated so uncertainly that the need was soon felt to introduce yet a further monetary unit: the so-called *lira a grossi*, which was designed to keep unchanged the old relation with the *grosso*. But while the first two types of money consisted of actual coins, this third type was used exclusively for calculation; it was a "money of account" or "ghost money", and was never turned into real coin. At Florence, after the creation of the florin, a similar unit of account was adopted: the *lira a fiorini*. This new "imaginary" money was used particularly in payments and exactions by the government, and in all kinds of contract which required an unambiguous measure of price, even though the sums involved were too small to warrant use of the *lira di grossi*.

Long before these developments, however, the rapid growth of Italian trade in the Mediterranean and western Europe had revealed the inadequacy of silver currency of any kind as a means of exchange; and this was felt all the more acutely because the gold coin of the Byzantines and Arabs no longer commanded confidence. Gold had never ceased to circulate as a medium of payment in Italian markets, but normally it took the form of gold bars of guaranteed weight and purity, or, more often, of Byzantine and Arab coin. It was only natural, therefore, when these foreign currencies became debased, that the Italian states in closest contact with the East should seek to replace them with a new gold coinage, which would gain universal acceptance. A start was made in 1231, when the Emperor Frederick II issued the *augustalis*, a gold coin with a fineness of $20\frac{1}{2}$ carats and a weight just over 6 grams. But not long after, *augustales* ceased to be struck, and in the event it fell to the Florentines to introduce the first truly successful gold coin. This was the celebrated florin, a coin of pure gold weighing 3·53 grams, which was issued for the first time in 1252 and soon won widespread recognition in the Mediterranean and all parts of the western world. The florin should have been equivalent to one pound of silver pennies, but in practice its value was officially raised, shortly after issue, to 29 shillings; and with the progressive deterioration of the small silver currency, this figure was retained as the standard rate of exchange between the florin and the *lira a fiorini*, or "money of account", referred to above.

In the same year 1252, shortly before or after Florence, Genoa also began to strike a gold coin, the *genoino*, though it did not have the same success as the florin. Venice, on the other hand, delayed some thirty years, down to 1284, before issuing its famous gold ducat (later called *zecchino*), which was another coin of pure gold, with a weight of 3·559 grams. The probable reasons for this delay were the reluctance of the Venetians to compromise their position in the Latin Empire by trying to impose a better coin than the debased hyperperon, and the desire to maintain a place in international trade for their silver *grosso*. But the situation changed with the fall of the Latin Empire. Not only did the Venetians lose their privileged status; the hyperperon rapidly fell to half its former value, while a *grosso* was issued at Constantinople which, although of baser alloy, was officially declared of equal value with the *grosso* of Venice. Further delay would have damaged Venetian trade. In the first few centuries the Venetian ducat was struck only in small quantities, but its stable weight and purity, which remained unchanged for 500 years, assured it complete and enduring success. Sufficient proof of its reputation are the many counterfeit and imitation ducats, which were issued with particular frequency, after the late fourteenth century, by the mints of the East.

Details about prices and wages, at various levels of society, abound in the records of many Italian towns, especially after the middle of the thirteenth century. But it would be pure illusion to suppose that we could ever compile a series of index numbers, to illustrate variations in the purchasing power of money during the later Middle Ages. What we can do, however, is estimate roughly the value of different rates of pay to those who received them, by comparing a comprehensive sample of salaries and wages with a few established facts about the cost of living.

Thus, to take just one or two examples, we know that at Florence, during the thirteen months between July 1290 and August 1291, the maintenance of two orphans, whose father had left them very modestly endowed, cost their guardian the sum of £21. 12s. *a fiorino*; that is to say, the approximate cost of boarding each of these two children for one year amounted to £10 *a fiorino* (bearing in mind that the florin was worth 29s.). Forty years later we find that, in a much higher sphere of Florentine society, the cost of keeping two young orphan girls of the Bardi family was assessed, apart from shoes and clothing, at £40 to £50 *piccoli*, or £20 to £25 per head. If we consider that by this time the exchange rate of the *piccolo* with the florin had fallen from 29*s.* to 62*s.*, then we must conclude that the two Bardi orphans cost no more to maintain than the two Ammannati wards.

Measured against these figures, the yearly salaries paid to representatives (*fattori*) of the Bardi company, which averaged £80 to £150 *a fiorino*, and often rose to more than £200 and even £300, would appear distinctly high. Not so, however, if we compare the same salaries with rents. In the first twenty years of the fourteenth century rents at Florence must have risen appreciably, with the rapid increase of population and economic activity. Yet even at the end of the thirteenth century, quite modest apartments were let, in two cases we know of, for more than £25 and £31 *a fiorino*, that is to say, for almost three times the cost of keeping a grown child in an upperclass family. The price of clothing also was considerably higher than the price of food. To provide a small gown for one of his wards, the guardian of the Ammannati spent £4 *a fiorino* on the cloth, which was certainly not of best quality, and another 5*s.* on dressmaking: altogether nearly half the cost of boarding the child for a full year.

Needless to say, salaries varied widely. Among the worst paid were schoolmasters, who received no more than 1*s.* 6*d.* a month for private lessons given in the pupil's home. A laundress got only 5*d.* for washing a pair of sheets. The rates of pay for doctors, on the other hand, were extremely high. A doctor hired by the commune, for service in a city ward, could draw between £50 and £120 *piccoli* per annum, and sometimes considerably more. Even so, these official salaries were small beside the private fees exacted by doctors at the top of their profession: in one case a famous practitioner charged 16 gold florins for a single treatment.

At Venice, towards the middle of the fourteenth century, the purchasing power of money was evidently much the same as at Florence. The yearly cost of subsistence (food and petty expenses) of an adult in the higher ranks of Venetian society was assessed in the courts of law at 15 to 20 gold ducats. There seems no reason to suppose that these judicial figures were far removed from reality; from certain executors' accounts of

1344–5 it appears that the cost of maintaining four brothers of noble family for the space of fifteen months amounted in all to 87 ducats, a total which yields an average of 15 ducats a year per person (treating children and adults alike). In Venice too we find a striking difference between the cost of food and the cost of clothing. Thus, with one *grosso* ($\frac{1}{24}$ of a gold ducat) it was possible to buy 3 lb. (*libre grosse*) of beef, or a goose, or 2 lb. of salted cheese, 1 litre of oil, more than 5 litres of wine, or 24 eggs (in April). The price of woollen cloth, by contrast, was 15 *grossi* a yard (*braccio*), so that the cost of material alone for clothing three children amounted to 15 gold ducats. Skin caps cost 4 *grossi* apiece. The rent of a house let to a doctor reached the figure of 30 ducats a year.

The price of services varied as much as the price of goods. In Venice, as in Florence, teachers were poorly paid. A master, employed as tutor to three children of a wealthy family, was granted 6 *grossi* a month, the same wage as a domestic servant, who was also given board and lodging, and a much lower wage than that of a children's nurse, who received in addition to maintenance one gold ducat a month. Conditions were slightly better perhaps for the masters of public schools, who drew 18 *grossi* a year in fees for each pupil. Even so, their situation was scarcely to be compared with that of the doctor of medicine who, for nine days' attendance on a rich patrician, received 9 gold ducats from the man's executors.

Among industrial workers at Venice, a privileged position was reserved to the caulkers, who worked as master craftsmen in the shipyards. Those employed in the Arsenal were paid 4 *grossi* and 40 *piccoli* per day during summer, and 3 *grossi* and 30 *piccoli* during winter; the corresponding rates for those employed in private shipbuilding were 6 *grossi* and 12 *piccoli*, 4 *grossi* and 12 *piccoli*. At first glance these wages would seem twice or three times the sum reputed necessary for the maintenance (without lodging) of a well-to-do Venetian citizen; but there is reason to think that part of the master caulker's pay was intended to provide the wages, scanty though they doubtless were, of two assistant workmen.

c. Credit

The complexity and diversity of the monetary system prevailing in the age of the communes, and the constant discrepancy existing between the monies of account used in business contracts and records and the currencies in actual circulation, compelled Italian merchants, from the early twelfth century on, to seek some alternative means of payment, both in local markets and abroad. For local business the method adopted was payment by transfer in bank, a system known already in the ancient world. For the transfer of money abroad the instruments devised were the contract and bill of exchange.

In the great commercial cities of Italy, France, Flanders, and England, and in the great international fairs, where banking remained an Italian monopoly for more than two centuries, bankers performed a public function, recording in their books the transfer of money from one client's account to another. At Venice, where this system was most widely adopted and all the greater merchants preferred to make their payments by "book transfer in the bank" (*scrivere e girare in banca*), banks themselves come to be known quite early by the name of "transfer banks" (*banchi de scripta*). Indeed, a large part of the international trade transacted at Venice was carried on in the tiny piazza of S. Giacomo di Rialto, where all the Venetian and foreign merchants, who kept an account with one or more of the local banks, would meet together regularly at their bank and conclude their business, often involving large transfers of money, by simple verbal order. This procedure by deposit and transfer offered two advantages: it made payment more easy and rapid, and it provided a money of account, later known as "bank money" (*moneta di banco*), which was treated as equivalent in value to the more reputable currencies. Despite its widespread use, this fiduciary money never circulated in the form of notes or any other kind of negotiable paper. It was certainly a common practice for bankers to issue their clients with tiny credit slips, recording their deposit in the bank, but there is nothing to show that in medieval Venice bankers' slips were used as a means of payment, as later became the custom in Sicily and southern Italy. Only in recent years have certain documents come to light in Florence which resemble modern cheques, but these still await proper study.

If medieval bankers had never done more than register (*scribere*) transfers of money in their books, they would not have been true bankers at all, but simply public officials, notaries specializing in one kind of work. But it is clear from numerous debates in the Maggior Consiglio of Venice that they were also in the habit of extending credit at legally recognized rates of interest. In these operations bankers must have employed not only their personal capital, but also such part of the money they held in deposit as their clients agreed to release for invest-ment and did not make repayable on request or short notice. So it was that, when the great Sienese banking house of the Bonsignori went bankrupt, the demand for total restitution of deposits was successfully resisted on the grounds that the clients had risked their money voluntarily.

An undoubted abuse, which certain medieval bankers were far too often ready to commit, was that of making payments on behalf of depositors whose credit balance did not cover them. In this way a fiduciary system of payments was established which was not secured by deposits of metal currency. As a result the value of "bank money" was undermined and eventually, as we shall see, some of the most reputable banks were brought to total ruin.

During the Middle Ages moneylending at interest was prac-tised not only by bankers and money-changers, but also, to an even greater extent perhaps, by merchants. To begin with merchants combined this activity with other kinds of business; but in course of time many turned to banking as their chief, and even exclusive, occupation. This was particularly true of three groups of merchants of different nationality, who acquired a monopoly of petty moneylending throughout the western world. The first were the Jews; the second were the so-called "Cahorsins", who derived their name from the town of Cahors in Gascony, but also included moneylenders from other parts of southern France and certain towns of Italy; and the third were the "Lombards" or "Tuscans", who consisted mainly of Piedmontese from Asti and Chieri, merchants from Piacenza, and Tuscans from Siena, Florence, and Pistoia.

The importance of the Jews in medieval moneylending is often exaggerated. During the barbarian and early feudal age, when they had been free to exploit their frequent contacts with the Byzantine, Arab, and eastern world, the Jews had played a leading part in trade between East and West. Some of them had been travelling merchants who accompanied their wares from place to place, but a number had also settled down permanently, in the south of France, the Iberian peninsula, and southern Italy, where beside commerce they took to industry and farming. What transformed the position of the Jews, before the outbreak of religious persecution, was the revival of towns and of urban economy. Under the communes industry and trade were limited to members of the guilds, and the guilds were Christian corporations which strictly excluded Jews. For a certain time the richer Jewish merchants were able to carry on business in long-distance trade, which was slower to submit to collective regulation. But gradually they were pushed out of this as well, and so found themselves restricted to dealing in second-hand goods and, more particularly, money. Only in certain parts of Italy, where craft and merchant guilds did not develop, did Jews retain any place in industry. Thus, Frederick II granted the Jews a monopoly of silk manufacture and dyeing throughout the kingdom of Sicily and Apulia, and two centuries later the dye industry of Apulia was still mainly in Jewish hands. But in most western countries, apart from Spain, the Jews were forced to realize their capital investments in land and industry, and assume the character of second-hand dealers and usurers; and even usury they were only allowed to practise in the form of petty pawnbroking.

Conditions were similar, though frequently far better, among the other groups of moneylenders, the Cahorsins and Lombards, who settled in the towns of France, England, and the Low Countries, and the Tuscans, whom we find recorded during the thirteenth century in numerous small centres of southern Italy, the Papal States, and eastern Venetia. Like the Jews, these men administered banks of very modest size and generally confined their operations to small loans for consumption, mostly on the pledge of personal property; but they also enjoyed an advantage over the Jews in having a government at home to which they could appeal for protection, and in being controlled or supported by some large commercial company, which could often give them the lucrative commission of administering the farm of certain taxes.

Far above these petty moneylenders stood the great commercial companies themselves, with their head offices in Rome, Siena, Florence, and Piacenza, and their local branches in all the leading cities of Italy, the Mediterranean, and western Europe. The agents of the big companies had first entered the western states as merchants attending the fairs of Champagne, or as papal tax-collectors. But they lost no time in developing the credit side of their business, choosing their clients for preference among the rulers and great lords. For many merchant bankers this policy ended in disaster, but in the meantime it secured them valuable trading privileges, especially in the export of English wool and French and Flemish cloth. Business grew so rapidly that firms were soon obliged to increase their initial capital, considerable though this was, either by raising additional funds from the partners of the company, or by taking money on deposit from outsiders, who demanded high rates of interest as partial compensation for their risks.

Of the various activities pursued by the big Italian companies, the lending of money at interest was the most profitable. In this connexion we must pause to consider the sharp contradiction existing in the Middle Ages between religious and moral principles, as formulated from an early date in the canonical prohibition of usury and embodied in the statutes of many urban communes, and the needs of daily life, which made recourse to borrowing unavoidable, even at the cost of having to pay very high rates of interest. So compelling were these practical needs that even the Church authorities were forced to abandon their extreme position and acknowledge that interest was proper in all cases where the lender exposed himself to demonstrable risk or loss, or loans were not repaid at maturity. In addition to this, a distinction was commonly drawn between productive loans, which were meant to make borrowers richer, and so-called consumption loans which made them poorer. On loans of the first class interest could be legitimately charged. These rules were not without some practical effect. From the fourteenth century on, interest rates became far less extortionate than they had been in the past, and if this change was mainly due to a greater abundance of money, it was also partly caused by the spread of these more liberal doctrines. Not that even now we can always speak of legal rates of interest, but interest rates often assumed an official character and only fluctuated with changes on the market. The urban communes were constantly obliged to turn to citizens or foreigners for short-term loans, on which the rates of interest varied during the thirteenth and fourteenth centuries from 7 per cent and 8 per cent to 12 per cent, and even occasionally 15 per cent. Private loans appear in the form of interest-free grants, lasting a month or (very rarely) a year, at the end of which interest was levied at the rate of 20 per cent per annum. If restitution was further delayed, the principal and interest were both doubled and the land or goods pledged in security were forfeited.

CHAPTER EIGHT

The Waning of the Middle Ages

I. THE CHANGING PLACE OF ITALY IN EUROPE AFTER 1350

WESTERN Europe was slow to discard the economic customs of the Middle Ages, and it is easy to form the impression that, in many parts of Europe at least, few changes of importance occurred before the later eighteenth century. Yet profound economic differences divided the sixteenth century from the Carolingian and feudal age. During the Middle Ages, in spite of the universal claims advanced by Papacy and Empire, most people passed their lives in the local seclusion of villages and manors, castles and townships. At no period perhaps did these small communities reach the position of total isolation and perfect self-sufficiency, of "closed" or "natural economy", which some historians have attributed to them; but certainly their economic life was extremely circumscribed, and their traffic with the outside world both difficult and infrequent. When we consider, further, the ban of the Church on usury and the doctrine that profits should be moderate and prices just, or recall the whole structure of corporate restraints on production and exchange, and the food regulations and agrarian policy of the towns, then we can properly appreciate the narrow limits and conservative spirit which confined and controlled medieval economic growth.

The gradual progress away from these conditions, which began in Italy during the twelfth century and gathered momentum in the two centuries following, may be traced in various spheres of economic life. Changes occurred in the trend and distribution of population. Larger territorial units were formed, which extended the range of local and foreign trade. In north and central Europe new peoples were brought within the orbit of commercial life, which for much of the Middle Ages had been almost closed to them. The domain of money economy was widened, and the production of precious metals was increased to meet the sharp rise in demand. Competition developed in Mediterranean trade from the merchants of Provence and Catalonia, while the trade itself was threatened by Turkish conquest in the East. Finally, voyages of geographical discovery were launched, though the full effect of these was only felt much later.

The trend of population seems to have been governed by much the same laws in medieval and early modern times, for in both periods, after a phase of steady increase, which was often prolonged, numbers sharply fell again until they reached roughly their original level. One cause of demographic decline was civil and foreign war, which laid whole regions waste, even though losses in battle were small. But the principal causes were famine and above all plague, which sometimes levied a fearful toll of lives. The most memorable and severe of medieval plagues was the Black Death, which spread from the Far East across the whole of Europe between 1347 and 1350, and inflicted terrible destruction on the population, especially in the towns. At Florence, for example, credible sources relate that three-quarters of the people died, and the shortage of labour in the woollen industry became so acute after 1349 that immigrant workers from distant places had to be employed.

In the period following 1350 the population must have started to rise again, though with varying intensity from region to region and subject to the usual fluctuations. But of greater general interest for economic history than the actual increase of population, which was limited down to the eighteenth century by the very high death-rate, were the changes which occurred in its local distribution. Thus, the urbanization of society which, until the fourteenth century, had been confined to a few areas of Mediterranean Europe, the North Sea, and the Baltic, now spread to new regions and assumed a new character. In Italy, with the rise of despotic states and principalities, which controlled relatively wide territory, certain of the larger cities began to exert a great force of attraction, not only on the villages and countryside, but also on the smaller towns, which had lost their independence. Thus in Venetia, after Venice had conquered the mainland, a number of flourishing towns, such as Padua and Verona, suffered depopulation as well as economic and political decline. Much the same occurred in Tuscany and Lombardy, to the profit of Florence and Milan, while in southern Italy Naples and Palermo absorbed the life of two entire regions.

The growth of large capital cities, which commanded far wider territory than the early communes possessed, was only one influence tending to transform and enlarge the closed economies of the past. Another was the spread of a money economy to countries which had previously occupied only a secondary place in the economic life of Europe. The consequent rise in demand for precious metals eventually outstripped production, and for a period of several decades, beginning in the thirteenth century, there were general complaints of a serious lack of silver. At other times gold became scarce. Only after 1450 did the search for new supplies of silver begin to yield measurable results, notably in Saxony and the Tyrol; while gold stocks were replenished by imports, first from the Urals by way of the Black Sea ports, and then from Africa by way of the Barbary ports.

In all directions the range of Italian commerce was steadily enlarged. To the east, we have already seen how merchant adventurers like the Polos travelled overland to China and parts of central Russia. We have also noted the thriving northern trade, which was carried on by Genoa, Milan, and still more Venice, with Poland and Germany. We must now record developments in the west, where enterprising mariners opened up new routes through the Straits of Gibraltar to Flanders and England, while a few bold navigators turned to the south, along the unexplored coasts of Africa, in search of new horizons or precious cargoes of slaves, gold, and other costly wares. The pioneers of African navigation were the Genoese captains, Tedisio Doria and the brothers Vivaldi, who in 1291 equipped two ships for a voyage of discovery beyond Cape Verde and the Gulf of Guinea. Their venture failed and nothing more was heard of them; but the Genoese were not discouraged, and early in the fourteenth century they succeeded in reaching the Canary Islands. Genoese seamen were also employed, along with a few Venetians, when the kings of Portugal began to develop African exploration systematically in the fifteenth century. It was now that voyages were organized, not simply for commercial gain, but also with the object of finding a sea-route to the Indies round the southernmost point of Africa. Not until 1484, however, did a Portuguese mariner, Bartolomeo Diaz, finally reach the Cape of Good Hope, and not until 1498 did Vasco da Gama round the Cape and sail to Calicut on the east coast of India. Meantime, in 1492, Christopher Columbus, in the service of Spain, had sailed across the Atlantic and, as he at first believed, successfully accomplished his mission of reaching the farthest shores of Asia.

As the range of commerce grew, so did the variety and volume of merchandise. The increase in volume was mainly due to the rising standard of living and to the entry into trade of European countries which until the thirteenth century had remained economically backward. The increase in variety, on the other hand, may be attributed partly to trade with new places, in Africa and elsewhere, and partly to the development of industries which needed large supplies of raw materials from abroad. Besides the usual traffic in eastern wares which had always been imported into Europe, we observe a revival of trade in slaves, especially slaves from Africa. Imports of precious metals also rose substantially, as we have seen; while the developing use of firearms added a new and powerful demand for imports of copper. Finally, increasing quantities of sugar and cotton were imported from India, Syria, and Egypt. Cotton was now being used much more extensively in the textile industry, while sugar, which had long been restricted to medicinal uses, was beginning to enter the home.

The expanding supply of goods from outside Europe was matched by expanding production inside Europe itself. Industry and agriculture were both affected, as well as all goods entering international trade, such as Italian silks and artistic wares, English woollen cloth and German mining and metal products, French wine and brandy, and the grain, flax, hemp, timber, and skins of the Baltic countries, Hungary, and Russia. Demand rose everywhere for high quality and luxury goods, as the refined manners and elegant tastes of princely courts and castles spread to the palaces and villas newly raised in large numbers, especially in Italy, by the wealthy middle class and urban patriciate. At the same time, however, the growth of a market for manufactures among people of humbler means created the need to cut down costs of production, in at least some ranges of goods, by sacrificing quality to quantity. This need was plainly recognized, from the very first years of the sixteenth century, by the Venetian ambassadors accredited to the various courts of Europe, who in their reports home repeatedly urged the government to encourage production of cheaper and coarser fabrics for the large new class of customers, and so defeat the challenge of foreign competition.

To the modern observer, who surveys this changing scene, it is clear that, from the final years of the fourteenth century, conditions were developing in Europe, which were destined eventually to bring decline upon the great cities of Italy. Economic influences apart, the Turkish danger in the East, the rise of united monarchies in the West, and the divided state of Italy itself, all combined to weaken resistance against the poor but powerful foreign states which coveted Italian wealth. And yet it would be wrong to conclude from these adverse circumstances that Renaissance Italy was in a state of unrelieved economic decay.

To be sure, many things had changed, both inside and outside the country. Gone was the time when Pisa, Genoa, and Venice could unconcernedly contend for control of the Mediterranean, without fear that other trade rivals would profit by their bitter conflicts. And gone was the time when Italian merchants virtually monopolized the banking and exchange business of France, England, and the Low Countries, and exploited their financial ascendancy to obtain commercial favours. In England, merchants and petty bankers were rising in revolt against Italian privilege, while in Flanders and France the first great financiers, such as the Arteveldes and Jacques Cœur, were coming to power. During the same period the largest Italian export industry of the fourteenth century began to exhibit disturbing symptoms of decline. At Florence the yearly output of woollen cloth, which had varied from 100,000 to 80,000 pieces in the early fourteenth century, had fallen to little more than 30,000 pieces a century later. The level of production, and sometimes of export, still remained high both at Florence and in certain other towns in Lombardy and Venetia; but apart from Florentine fabrics, Italian cloth exports were now in process of losing the position they had held for almost two hundred years in the wealthy markets of the East. To meet the demands of eastern buyers, even the Venetians had to place their orders with Flemish or English merchants and artisans. The Venetians, in fact, were among the most faithful customers of these northern producers.

Not only the woollen industry declined but also, on a smaller scale, the fustian industry, which had formerly flourished at Cremona, Chieri, and other towns in Lombardy and Piedmont, but after the fifteenth century was compelled to face formidable competition from the cities of Upper Germany. Another case is Milan, which under the Visconti and the early Sforza was the main Italian centre of the metal industry, but subsequently became dependent on the German town of Nuremberg for many products of the very same branch of industry.

Even in the Mediterranean the mercantile supremacy of Italy was challenged by the towns of southern France, and even more by the Catalans, who from their bases in the Balearics, Sardinia, and Sicily extended their activities as far as the Levant.

By the fifteenth century, it is obvious, Italy no longer occupied the same place in the economy of Europe as in the two preceding centuries. The old position of monopoly was gone, and the old power of expansion was enfeebled. To this extent, undoubtedly, it is proper to speak of Italian economic decline. But to use the word "decline" in the further sense, of an absolute fall in the volume and value of production and exchange, would be wholly unjustified. Indeed, with very few exceptions, production and exchange were quite unaffected when the Italians lost their monopoly, and sometimes even their leading place, in the several branches of medieval commerce. If production for export contracted in the woollen industry, the loss was largely balanced by compensating progress in the silk industry, which during the late fourteenth and early fifteenth centuries spread from southern Italy, and still more, Lucca, where silk manufacture had first developed and prospered, to the cities of Florence, Bologna, Venice, Milan, and Genoa.

Admittedly, the industry never became important for the number of people it employed, but the value of its products was inestimable. During the fifteenth century court life in Italy attained its highest point of splendour. The cult of gentle living, and the taste for art, letters, and luxury, invaded not only the palaces of princes and wealthy merchants, but also the castles of countless petty lords and despots, who ruled the small states of central Italy or clung to independent power elsewhere. For the proper appointment of these lordly palaces and castles, as well as of the churches, silks were judged as necessary as paintings, frescoes, and marble sculptures. Silk no longer served merely for dress or sacred vestments, but also for decoration. This was why the production of damasks and brocades, with interwoven silk, gold, and silver thread, was rapidly expanded and perfected.

Not only the manufacture of silk was stimulated by the new love for luxury, elegance, and artistic refinement. All industries were affected which produced articles for personal adornment or the embellishment of the home and public and religious buildings. Handicrafts in wood and iron, copper, bronze, precious stones and metals, glass manufacture and ceramics, embroidery and lace-making, these and similar trades all began to flourish, especially in the large commercial centres, where they provided a regular and remunerative means of payment for imported raw materials.

For more than a century the preeminence of Renaissance Italy in the manufacture of artistic and luxury wares helped to maintain Italian foreign trade at much the same level as in the most prosperous period of the past, and may even have raised it higher. While the volume of traffic amply compensated Italian merchants for the loss of their one-time monopoly, the enhanced value of their exports and the better opportunities offered for their banking and credit operations enabled them to amass large fortunes at a faster rate than before. It may be true that Renaissance Italy did not boast any world-famous business house as important as the House of Fugger; but long before the rise of the Fugger, and throughout the period that witnessed their expansion and decline, there were dozens of firms in Italy transacting similar business of a comparable magnitude over just as large an area. Notwithstanding the profound crisis which overtook the great banking houses of Florence in the middle of the fourteenth century, and spread, about the same time, to other towns in Italy, Italian banking did not cease to function, but rather revealed, in the two succeeding centuries, remarkable powers of recovery. According to one chronicler, reliably informed in economic matters, there were thirty-two banking firms at Florence in 1470, of which at least a dozen handled business equal or superior to that of their fourteenth-century predecessors, while at least three (the Medici, the Pazzi, and after the Pazzi fell, the Strozzi) wielded power of truly world-wide dimensions, devoting to high finance two or three times as much capital as the Bardi and Peruzzi.

But if Florence, in the early sixteenth century, was still the town of Italy with the greatest private fortunes, or, at any rate, the greatest number of wealthy family partnerships, other towns were not very far behind. In Tuscany itself there were Lucca and Siena which, although much decayed since the thirteenth century, could still produce families of the first rank in international commerce and finance. Indeed, it was a Sienese banker, Agostino Chigi, who during the pontificate of Alexander VI and Julius II displaced the Medici and Pazzi from the management of papal finances, supplanted the Medici in the lucrative farm of the Tolfa alum mines, and built himself a fortune reputed the largest in the whole of Italy. At Prato, finally, Francesco di Marco Datini developed a vast, complex business, with numerous subsidiaries in Italy and western Europe.

During the fifteenth century certain Genoese families began to acquire commanding influence in the world of high finance, notably the Spinola, the Centurioni, the Giustiniani, and the Doria. They reached the height of their power in the sixteenth century when, in concert or competition with the great bankers of Upper Germany, they invested enormous sums in all the major financial projects from Lisbon to Antwerp. After the collapse of the Fugger, they became the principal financiers of the kings of Spain, while the Florentines rendered corresponding services to the kings of France.

In Lombardy too a number of merchants and bankers achieved more than local importance at this time. We may mention particularly the Affaitati of Cremona, who took a share in Portuguese trade with the Indies between 1501 and 1503, and subsequently established a flourishing factory at Antwerp. Or again there were the Borromei, a Tuscan family from San Miniato, who moved to Milan in the fifteenth century and within a short time succeeded in creating a prosperous business with independent branches of high repute at Venice, Bruges, and London.

Venice, for various reasons, was never able to compete with Florence or Genoa in financial dealings with foreign powers. For one thing, the Venetian government was in too frequent need of funds for the struggle with the Turks, for the ruinous wars waged on the Italian mainland, and for the upkeep of the navy and merchant marine. For another, the Venetian aristocracy always viewed with suspicion excessive concentrations of wealth and power in the hands of one family. Bankers naturally there were, some of whom handled an impressive volume of business; but the business they handled was almost entirely absorbed by the domestic needs of Venetian commerce and even more perhaps of the Venetian state. Thus, to take one example, the Soranzo bank, which must have been one of the largest, continued for over fifty years, until its fall in 1491, to make substantial and repeated advances of credit to the Signoria, for sums often exceeding 10,000 ducats and sometimes amounting to as much as 80,000. Presumably these were all short-term transactions, but repayments were so dilatory that the bank was left with insufficient capital at its disposal and finally went bankrupt. Much the same fate befell other great Venetian banking houses, such as the Gazzoni, Veruzi, Priuli, and Lippomano.

We should not regard the rise of great families to new wealth, the lavish investment of wealth in new building and patronage, or the spread of a new artistic sensibility and higher level of culture, as the sole characteristics of economic life in Renaissance Italy. Beside these indications of progress or prosperity we have to set the clear and constant evidence of peasant poverty and proletarian destitution, as well as the tendency, which has often been exaggerated but undoubtedly existed, for some members of the new aristocracy of money to withdraw their capital from industry and trade and invest it, from motives of security and social prestige, in town and country properties. But it must be pointed out that neither of these facts was new. It may be that rural poverty became more painfully apparent in the presence of the palaces and villas which were now being built, and of the life of luxury displayed in them; but peasant conditions were certainly no better in the thirteenth century, when the frugal habits of the rising middle class concealed social contrasts more effectively. The practice of transferring capital from business to land was equally old, as old in fact as the existence of a moneyed middle class. At Venice, as early as the thirteenth century, when the commune still possessed no territory beyond the fringe of the lagoons, merchants were busy buying up estates on the nearby mainland, despite the risks of owning property in foreign and often unfriendly states. At Florence, in the fourteenth century, the depositors and creditors of the bankrupt Bardi, Peruzzi, and other banking families, were able to recover a fair proportion of their claims, just because the assets of these firms included landed property, which the partners had acquired with part of their profits, or possessed by some older title.

2. THE GREAT SEA POWERS: GENOA AND VENICE

To the contemporary, who looked no further than the main centres of economic life, Renaissance Italy appeared as a land of abounding prosperity and exuberant wealth; so much so that the coveted riches of Italy were not the least cause of her misfortune. Yet a closer view of the country as a whole soon reveals pronounced regional differences.

It would be natural to think that the great maritime towns, especially Genoa and Venice, which for full two hundred years had enjoyed world-wide preeminence, would have been the first to suffer from the changing economic situation. At the beginning of the fifteenth century political conditions in these two cities were profoundly different. Both, it is true, had emerged from the War of Chioggia cruelly prostrated, but Genoa was far more lastingly affected by the struggle than Venice. In particular, Venice succeeded in maintaining her position as an independent sovereign state, notwithstanding the threatening advance of the Ottoman Turks and the increasing financial difficulties arising from a policy of war and expansion on the mainland. At Venice the inevitable conflicts of ambition and interest among the greater noble families never compromised the unity or authority of the state; the crafts and petty trade guilds, far from becoming an instrument of revolution to the classes excluded from power, were strictly and successfully controlled as an instrument of domination by the classes possessed of power; finally, the growing dependence of the state on borrowing and credit was never allowed to limit its full financial sovereignty. The Venetians managed their foreign relations with equal competence. Not only did they keep control of the Adriatic, but they also contrived, by a prudent policy of intermittent war and treaty with the Turks, to save their possessions in Cyprus, Crete, and the Aegean Sea, at least until the middle of the sixteenth century, and to safeguard their trade with the eastern Mediterranean and even with Constantinople itself. At sea, the Venetians maintained the strongest navy in southern Europe; on land, they advanced their dominions from the Adriatic coast to the Adda, from Friuli to the Polesine, and for a time even further, to Ravenna; and in the politics of Italy they achieved such a powerful influence as to justify the fear that they planned to dominate the whole peninsula.

Genoa, by contrast, seems to have expended her last reserves of political strength in the final contest with Venice. The city was afflicted by faction at home and assailed by rivalries abroad, in the western Mediterranean: by the old rivalry of Marseilles, by the new rivalry of Florence, which followed the conquest of Pisa, and most of all, by the preponderant power of the Aragonese. For Genoa this was a period of prolonged and critical decline, in which a bankrupt government was forced to surrender its most valued prerogatives in order to discharge its financial obligations. The public debt had so increased that the holders of government securities had now to be granted, not only the right to collect certain taxes, but also the authority to administer certain colonies, and even, eventually, certain territories in Liguria itself; and when, in 1407, the bondholders united in a single organization, the Casa di S. Giorgio, they came to constitute nothing less than a rival state within the state, accroaching to themselves extensive powers of government in the city, its colonies and dominions. But an even clearer proof of weakness in the Genoese state was its loss of independence by repeated submission to the rule or protectorate of foreign powers: first of France, then of Milan, and finally of Spain.

Yet the decay of Genoese political and military power, and the loss of the Genoese colonies in the Black Sea and the Levant, were not accompanied by any rapid decline in the prosperity of Genoese merchants and shippers. On the contrary, they seem almost to have profited by the failure of public authority. Private enterprise flourished and private fortunes continued to be made, especially in shipping and banking. In the case of shipping the contrast of public poverty and private wealth was particularly evident; for while the government had to cut down its naval strength to a minimum and could sometimes barely muster half a dozen galleys, there were some private owners who could comfortably equip larger war fleets than the state. A few of these men maintained private navies more for profit than for power, hiring out their ships to foreign rulers on the best terms they could get, and setting up in business as *condottieri* of the sea. Needless to say, this was not the only type of maritime activity that prospered on the busy coasts of Liguria. The Genoese were bold, enterprising, and expert seamen, who were ready to sail in any direction for a profitable charter or cargo. The countries of their preference were Spain and Portugal, where they rendered priceless services in preparing and launching the first voyages of discovery, which were destined to revolutionize long-distance trade by sea.

Besides shipping in all its forms, late medieval Genoa also witnessed the development of various types of capitalistic enterprise, ranging from industries like shipbuilding and silk manufacture to banking and foreign exchange. For shipbuilding, which by its very nature required heavy capital investment, Liguria had the advantage of commanding supplies of highly skilled labour, especially along the eastern coast (Riviera di Levante); at the same time there was plenty of demand from private shipowners, as well as from states and customers overseas, to compensate for the falling demand of the Genoese government. As for silk manufacture, this underwent a great expansion, at Genoa as everywhere else, during the fifteenth century; the industry was organized upon a handicraft basis, but being entirely controlled by the silk merchants, it gradually assumed under their direction a capitalistic character. Not industry, however, but banking and credit were the most regular and rewarding forms of investment for the capital accumulated by the Genoese in several centuries of international trade. Credit operations included loans to the Genoese government, and later, on a larger scale, to the government of Spain. In addition to this, however, Genoese bankers made a special business of exchange, which eventually they came to dominate in sixteenth-century Europe, and which they found a convenient cover for many kinds of loan contract and speculation.

The history of Genoese capitalism is inseparable from the history of the large and ever-increasing Genoese public debt, since the debt, as we have seen, was responsible for the foundation of the famous Casa di S. Giorgio or "Firm of St. George". This "firm" was established by a law of 1405, and began operations in 1407, under the name of "Company of the tax concessions and banks of St. George" (*Societa delle compere e dei banchi di San Giorgio*). The name is somewhat misleading, for the Casa was not a true business company so much as an institution charged with the independent management of the national debt. It resembled a company in this, however, that the representatives of the state were finally excluded by the representatives of the shareholders. It was also to protect the shareholders, and guarantee payment of their interest, that the Casa was entrusted, at its inception, with control of the salt monopoly and various gabelles, and later on, as loans to the government multiplied, with the administration of certain castles and territories belonging to the state, as well as certain overseas possessions such as Corsica. In addition to managing the public debt, the Casa was further authorized, in 1408, to act as a bank, on the understanding, however, that it limited its dealings to the business of deposit and transfer, and to granting credit to tax-farmers and the state. The bank's affairs grew rapidly, and in 1439 it opened two subsidiary branches; but all profits were reserved to the sinking fund. At the same time the banking department of the Casa was expected to regulate the circulation of money. But this activity was compromised by the government, which insisted, at a certain point, that the bank should try to stop the steady deterioration of the Genoese pound by giving it a higher value than was quoted on the market. This obligation exposed the Casa to such a serious risk of loss, that in 1444 the directors decided to surrender their concession and close down the bank altogether. It was not reestablished until 1586.

Between Renaissance Genoa and Renaissance Venice the differences, as we have said, were profound. As a maritime people, who continued to regard the sea as the principal foundation of their wealth, power, and very existence, the Venetians devoted all their care to defending the position they had won during 400 years of tenacious endeavour. They could never relax their vigilance, and even in the years of peace, when they managed by adroit diplomacy to avoid open conflict with the Turks, they had to keep a well-armed fleet of galleys at sea, to preserve respect for their authority and uphold their prestige in the Adriatic and Aegean. This arduous policy imposed on them a programme of naval construction, armament, and recruitment, which very few states of the time could have afforded to maintain. Nor was this all, for at the same time that they were successfully fighting the effects of the Ottoman advance to Constantinople, the Venetians also embarked on a rapid and triumphant conquest of the neighbouring mainland, extending the frontiers of their state to the west of Lake Garda and south of the Adige and lower Po. Their motive was not ambition for territorial aggrandizement, but a mortal fear of being cut off from their land communications with the Po valley and the countries beyond the Alps, by powerful princes like the Carraresi, Scaligeri, and—most dangerous of all—the Visconti, who threatened to unite in one hostile dominion the entire Venetian hinterland. The effect of territorial conquest was to embroil Venice in the ceaseless wars of the Italian states, wars which not only compromised and complicated the life-and-death struggle with the Turks, but frequently imposed still heavier financial sacrifices than the Turkish war itself. And yet the Venetians managed to bear these burdens. Indeed, they mastered difficulties which would have seemed to challenge the resources of far stronger states, and their powers of resistance were astonishing. They even emerged without disastrous loss from the War of Cambrai, the most deadly threat to Venetian independence since the War of Chioggia.

It must also be observed that, despite the demands of government finance, the extraordinary levies and incessant forced loans, Venice continued to enjoy the reputation of a wealthy city, the wealthiest in Italy and possibly in Europe. The Venetian chronicler, Marin Sanudo, who knew his city well, refers with pride to the large numbers of new palaces which were starting to crowd the Grand Canal and other waterways of Venice; to the systematic rebuilding of streets and bridges, and the exquisite works of art with which churches and public buildings were being enriched, without regard for cost; to the dazzling variety of goods on display beneath the porticoes of the Rialto, in the Mercerie and the weekly markets of S. Marco and S. Polo; to the high rent of shops and houses; to the priceless jewels and finery of Venetian women. But what he most admires is the profusion of foodstuffs and other necessities with which Venice was ceaselessly supplied.

"In this land", he writes, "where nothing grows, you will find an abundance of everything; for all manner of things from every corner and country of the earth which has stuff to send, especially food, are brought to this place; and there are plenty to buy, since everyone has money. The Rialto looks like a garden, such a wealth there is of herbs and vegetables from the places nearby, such an endless variety of fruits and all so cheap, that it is wonderful to see."

It is true that Sanudo wrote these words of his precious *Cronachetta* some fifteen years before the War of Cambrai; but Sansovino has similar things to say a century later, and in the early years of the seventeenth century the Calabrian, Antonio Serra, still pronounces Venice the first town in Italy for riches and trade. If the great merchants of southern Germany were now drawn to Lisbon and Antwerp, and trade with the Levant was often interrupted by war, the Fondaco dei Tedeschi, or "German factory" in Venice, remained for many years a busy centre of affairs, busier perhaps than at any time before. Though the building was destroyed by fire in 1505, it was quickly re-erected, and on a far grander scale than in the past. To be sure, the Venetian market was not what it had been one or two centuries earlier; the Levant trade, and most other trade outside the Adriatic, showed alarming symptoms of decline, and as early as 1506 a special board of commissioners was established, the Cinque Savi alla Mercanzia, whose main purpose it was to suggest ways and means of revival. No doubt the seasonal convoys were still despatched to the ports of Syria and Alexandria, but except in a few favourable years, when the Cairo and Damascus caravans were more richly laden than usual, the number of craft employed must have been very small. Venetian ships were no longer allowed past the Straits, and in certain years they even failed to reach Constantinople. The Flanders convoys also could rarely find contractors, despite the generous bounties offered by the state, and in a short time they had to be abandoned. Broadly speaking, the only overseas goods still entering Venice in quantity came from the Adriatic, Ionian, and Aegean ports, or from Crete and Sicily. At the same time fewer goods were leaving Venice, for the decline of Venetian seaborne trade was accompanied by a falling-off in Venetian exports of Italian industrial products. The countries of the Levant, which at one time Venice had supplied with a great part of Florentine and north Italian cloth, were now buying English, French, and Flemish cloth, and this travelled less and less by way of Venice. Nor were Italian silks, however sumptuous, any substitute for woollen cloth, for eastern markets certainly had silk in plenty.

Yet, despite all this, Venice remained a vigorous centre of foreign trade, frequented by merchants from every part of Italy and Europe; and the *piazzetta* of S. Giacomo di Rialto continued to be enlivened every morning by all the activity of an international stock market, where the prices of government bonds and foreign currencies, pepper and other spices, were eagerly quoted and exchanged. This was partly the effect of tradition, of inherited fame and commercial organization. It was also partly a consequence of Venetian policy towards foreigners, who although subjected to serious restrictions in the interest of Venetian citizens and Venetian public finance, were always assured of complete personal security and a rigorous protection of their legal rights and interests. But there were stronger reasons than these why foreigners still came crowding to Venice. One was the richness of the market itself, which despite declining imports of spices still displayed a great profusion and variety of merchandise from overseas. Another was the ease with which goods and money could be transferred from Venice at all possible times to all possible places. But the greatest attraction of all was the undiminished importance of Venice as a centre of foreign exchange. The Fugger, for example, throughout their career, maintained an important branch of their business at Venice, and this they did for two main reasons: because Venice offered the most convenient means of distributing the copper and other products of their mines, and because the Venetian or Tuscan and other Italian banks with branches in the city provided the best facilities for collecting and remitting funds to Rome and the other principal markets of Europe.

Not the least potent influence on Venetian trade were the needs of Venice itself, which probably maintained a higher standard of living than any other city in Europe. The Venetian ambassadors, for instance, comment with surprise, not to say pity, on the very sober habits of the Florentine nobility and upper middle class, and they frequently poke fun at the meanness of the Spaniards. Very different were the manners of their own citizens, as described already by Sanudo at the end of the fifteenth century. The Venetian mode of life demanded stately palaces in every corner of the city, a profusion of shops selling jewellery, perfumes, costly ornaments and fabrics, a large population of household slaves and courtesans, and—most significant of all—a copious supply of grain, oil, and other foodstuffs, especially vintage wines, from Crete, the coasts of Asia Minor, and various parts of Italy.

Venetian family fortunes in the fifteenth and early sixteenth centuries are much less precisely and generously documented than the private wealth of the Florentines; but we can learn something from certain fifteenth-century chroniclers, who possessed a precocious interest in economic problems. Of particular importance is the evidence of Malipiero concerning the personal wealth of Andrea Vendramin and Francesco Balbi—evidence which incidentally belies the common assertion that, from the second half of the fifteenth century, Venetian nobles were giving up trade for investment in landed property and the comforts of a quiet life. Malipiero relates that Andrea Vendramin, at the time of his election as doge, possessed a private fortune of 160,000 gold ducats and had assigned to each of his six daughters a marriage portion of 7,000 ducats. As for the sources of these riches, Malipiero explains that, during his early life, Vendramin had engaged in foreign trade, and that in partnership with his brother Luca he had been accustomed to provide a cargo of one and a half or two complete galleys, each of which was valued in money and goods at a total of 200,000 ducats; he had also employed a large number of agents who had grown rich in his service, including two members of the nobility, Giacomo Malipiero and Pietro Morosini. Of Francesco Balbi, who died in 1470 at the age of eighty four, Malipiero says that he stayed in business till the very last days of his life, that he was owner of a bank, and that his wealth enabled him to fit out three entire Flanders galleys with his own unaided resources.

The conquest of the mainland clearly did not cause the Venetians to turn away from commerce. Nor, as we have seen, did it suddenly start them buying up land, for this they had always done. There can be no doubt, however, that by flooding the market with the properties of dispossessed despots and rebels, the conquest did encourage the Venetian nobility to acquire large estates, and that it did confront the Venetian government with quite new problems concerning the drainage of land and river regulation, agriculture, mining, and forestry. At first these problems were dealt with individually as they arose, but in course of time special departments were set up which accomplished valuable work in controlling rivers and reclaiming swamp, building roads, promoting new crops, and protecting woodland.

But the main concern of Venetian economic policy in these years was not so much to exploit the mainland as to encourage, for the first time, the development of industries, which would nourish the export trade and replace as far as possible the failing supplies of manufactured goods from Italy and abroad. After the end of the fifteenth century these foreign supplies dried up almost completely. The chronicler Priuli relates that in 1495–6 the Syrian convoy (*muda*) put to sea with 50,000 ducats in cash, 30,000 lb. of copper, and a fair amount of miscellaneous merchandise, but hardly any woollen cloth; he also states that the Alexandrian galleys set out with 190,000 ducats in cash, 1,100,000 lb. of copper, and 500 casks of wine, but in this case he does not refer to cloth or manufactures at all. Now that the principal reason for admitting foreign textiles freely had gone, the government could give more willing attention to the demands of local producers; and so for the first time a protectionist policy was introduced into Venice. It worked to such purpose that, in the short space of fifty years, between 1516 and 1569, the output of cloth rose twentyfold (from 1,306 to 26,539 pieces). Other growing export industries were silk and glass manufacture, and artistic work in leather, wood, and metals. Even the printing industry had a certain economic importance, for during the sixteenth century Venice became one of the leading centres in Europe of publishing and typography.

3. TOWN AND COUNTRY IN LOMBARDY AND TUSCANY

The tenacious vitality of the great Italian sea powers down to the end of the sixteenth century inevitably affected those inland areas by tradition most closely bound to them. This was particularly evident in Lombardy, which was favourably placed for communications, not only with Venice by the natural highway of the Po, but also with Genoa by at least two good passes over the Apennines, and with Switzerland, the Rhineland, and Bavaria by numerous negotiable routes across the central Alps. The famous deathbed speeches ascribed by the chronicler Sanudo to the doge Tomaso Mocenigo contain precise and emphatic evidence that, by the early fifteenth century, Lombardy had assumed the dominant place in Venetian foreign trade, and that in particular the woollen industry of many Lombard cities and the fustian industry of Cremona had both reached an impressive level of production. Mocenigo says that Lombardy (which at that time included Novara, Alessandria, and Piacenza, but not the Valtellina) was accustomed to send to Venice on a yearly average 1,600,000 gold ducats, besides 48,000 pieces of woollen cloth and 40,000 pieces of fustian, amounting in value to 900,000 ducats more. A simple calculation shows that, with customs duty added, the total of sales and purchases by Lombard merchants in Venice, combined with the costs of storage and packing, represented no less than a quarter or more of all Venetian trade as estimated by Mocenigo. These statistics may be treated as roughly accurate, on analogy with other details in the same source relating to government finance, the public debt and the Arsenal, which can be independently confirmed. The figures are important not merely as absolute quantities, but even more for the comparison they enable us to make between conditions in the major economic centres of Lombardy, and between these and other towns in Italy. Thus it appears that, although Florence surpassed all other places in the volume of its trade with Venice, exporting there some 16,000 pieces of fine and medium quality cloth, the Lombard towns collectively left Florence far behind, at least in quantity of cloth, with a total export to Venice of 48,000 pieces. All the Lombard towns took a share in this trade, except Piacenza: Como with 12,000 pieces, Monza with 6,000, Brescia with 5,000, Pavia with 3,000. Milan contributed only 4,000 pieces, but in the quality of its cloth easily outdistanced all the smaller towns; the price of Milanese cloth was 30 ducats the piece, while the other Lombard woollens fetched only 15 ducats the piece or, in the case of Bergamasque cloth, which was the coarsest of all, a mere 7 ducats the piece. The town of Cremona is mentioned only for its fustians—40,000 pieces in all—and seems to have been the sole exporter to Venice of this type of fabric. The reliability of these statistics is confirmed by other details, which Mocenigo gives, showing the large quantities of raw materials, especially dyestuffs, raw and spun cotton, and French and Spanish wool, which the Lombards bought in Venice and which almost equalled in value the cloth they exported there.

The industrial activity of Milan and the other Lombard cities, described in Mocenigo's report and other sources of the Visconti and Sforza period, was a product primarily of trade. For it was during this period that Lombardy, and preeminently Milan, became the natural focus of all overland trade passing between the Po valley, Genoa, Tuscany, and, to a less extent, every other part of Italy, and the countries of central Europe. To this concentration of traffic Lombardy still owes its great commercial prosperity, and in the later Middle Ages, as today, trade was the major stimulus of industry, and even indirectly of agriculture. The textile industries came first in importance, although from the late fifteenth century Lombard woollens and fustians began to suffer damaging competition, at least in markets abroad, from foreign cloth manufacturers (whose principal agents at this time were the Italian merchants themselves). At Cremona, for example, we find the city magistrates supporting a petition for reduced taxation with the statement that since the beginning of Spanish rule the number employed in the fustian industry had fallen from 12,000 to only 440; although they overstated their case, it is certain that the industry had been disastrously hit by competition from the towns of upper Germany. More promising was the progress we have noted already in the silk industry. And this was not the only industry to prosper in late medieval Lombardy. Metallurgy also rapidly expanded, especially in the branch of arms production. The demand for armaments was continually increasing, and the greatest centre of their manufacture and export became Milan.

Side by side with industry and trade, agriculture also prospered, at least in certain parts of Lombardy, notably the lower plain. New crops were introduced and disseminated: mulberries in the upper plain and hills, rice in the lower Milanese and Lomellina; flax was grown in larger quantities, and also fodder crops, which enabled farmers to keep more cattle and fewer sheep and pigs. But the most revealing sign of a new interest in agriculture was the increasing care devoted by communes, princes, and great proprietors to the work of regulating streams, building canals, and draining and irrigating the lower Lombard plain. The prodigious achievement of reclaiming the land between the line of lowland springs (*risorgive*) and the left bank of the Po, which has transformed an almost unbroken expanse of heath, marshy undergrowth, and swamp into one of the most intensively and scientifically cultivated areas in Europe, was not accomplished in a single generation or century; more likely it occupied thousands of years. And progress was not continuous. After a long period of neglect, when the enterprise of earlier ages was completely undone, the work was resumed about the turn of the tenth century and pursued with increasing energy under the communes, the Visconti, and the Sforza. In the short space of thirty-six years, between 1439 and 1475, 55 miles of navigable canal, equipped with 25 locks, were constructed in the country south of Milan; and these canals fed numerous lesser waterways and ditches for irrigation. Even now the work was incomplete, but at least a decisive step had been made towards redeeming lowland Lombardy for farming.

In Tuscany, economic development took a different course in north and south. The southern region, which was united under Sienese rule, now lost practically all its earlier importance in the world of banking and international trade, while its various provinces, in particular the semi-desolate Maremma, now came to form an agricultural hinterland, providing Tuscan and Ligurian cities with farm produce and livestock. Meanwhile, northern Tuscany—with the sole exception of Lucca—was gradually subjugated by the Florentines, who in 1405, by the conquest of Pisa and Bocca d'Arno, finally realized their ancient ambition to dominate the whole Arno valley and command an independent outlet to the sea. At first, the conquest yielded only limited advantages, because the Pisan authorities, shortly before capitulation, had invested the Genoese with Porto Pisano and the castle of Leghorn with its tiny port. But the Florentines were not discouraged, and after fifteen years of waiting, they were able to profit by the weakness of the Genoese government and secure with money what they had failed to secure with arms.

Florence now devoted every effort to becoming a maritime power. In the very year of the Genoese purchase (1421), six Consuls of the Sea (*Consoli del mare*) were appointed, three at Florence and three at Pisa, who were charged to provide, among other things, for the construction of merchant-galleys in the Arsenal of Pisa, and to hire them out for the various trading-voyages fixed each year by the government. Adopting Venetian practice, Florence proceeded to establish three regular convoys to Alexandria, Constantinople, Bruges, and Southampton, with subsidiary voyages to the Barbary coast, Sicily, and Catalonia. By 1426 the system was in full operation. And yet, despite the lavish care of the Florentine government, it was never destined to prosper. Within a very few years the government had to reduce the size and number of convoys, and instead of drawing revenue from the sale of shipping contracts, it was compelled to vote a subsidy of 15,000 gold florins for the period of five years, in order to ensure a skeleton service of two yearly galleys to Flanders and one to Constantinople. Not even the subsidy, however, was enough to induce Florentine capitalists to face the risk of these maritime speculations; and as early as 1441 it was decided that, failing offers from private contractors, the *Consoli del mare* should despatch the boats entirely at public expense. In addition to this, special concessions were granted to foreigners who shipped their goods in Florentine state galleys. But it was all to no purpose. After several years the convoys to one destination or the other had to be suspended. The system of state navigation was clearly breaking down. In 1465, faced with the growing shortage of overseas merchandise, the government was forced to grant full freedom of trade to all Florentine and foreign shipping. Matters even reached the point that, in 1480, the state convoys were suppressed outright for four years and the *Consoli del mare* forbidden to build new ships. In the end, therefore, after sixty years of discouraging experiment, Florence had to abandon the attempt to become a sea power—at least in the sense then understood, of a state which, for purposes of profit, constructed and also often equipped its own merchant fleet, and controlled and directed the movement of overseas trade.

But although unsuccessful in exploiting the conquest of Pisa and the decline of Genoa to become a great naval power, and although weakened by the disastrous bank failures of 1345 and the plague of 1348, Florence continued throughout the Renaissance period to enjoy extreme prosperity and preserve an undisputed place among the greatest cities of Italy and Europe. This position she owed not only to the enterprise and versatility of her great merchant bankers, but also, in declining measure, to her important export industries. It is certainly true that the largest Florentine industry, the woollen industry, was condemned at the time to see its markets increasingly restricted, partly by foreign competition, partly by competition from neighbouring towns like Prato, Pistoia, Bologna, Lucca, and Pisa, and even smaller centres like San Gimignano and San Miniato. The Ciompi rising of 1378 seems to have been encouraged by critical conditions in the industry, for one demand of the insurgents was that the wool masters should be compelled to produce a minimum of 24,000 pieces of cloth each year. As it turned out, the rising only made the situation worse, by forcing large numbers of proscribed or politically tainted workers to seek asylum in other towns, like Padua, where they helped rival industries to grow. Early in the fifteenth century, however, these losses were redressed, at least in part, by a heavy immigration of textile workers from Flanders. Some indication that the industry was starting to revive after 1420 may be found in the great stress placed on imports of English wool in the discussions concerning convoys to the northern seas. The reports of the *Consoli del mare* at Pisa on the goods entering Porto Pisano reveal that the two galleys which returned from the western voyage on 16 June 1466 brought a cargo containing no less than 2,253 bales of raw wool, as compared with a mere 64 bales of cloth, 200 bars of lead, and a negligible quantity of tin and other commodities. Each bale of wool was valued at 50 gold florins, and each probably weighed 160 kilograms, making a total of 360 tons of raw wool, all of which was presumably destined for the manufacture of the best quality Florentine cloth. But although the industry revived, and the number of wool firms rose from 180 in 1427 to 270 in 1480, it does not appear that production ever exceeded 30,000 pieces at any time during the fifteenth century. So when the doge Mocenigo states, in 1421, that Florentine merchants imported 15,000 pieces to Venice every year, it can only be assumed that part of this cloth was manufactured in other towns of Tuscany.

The ageing industry held out in face of mounting difficulties down to the early sixteenth century, and as late as 1527 an expert observer could still assess the annual output at 19,000 pieces of cloth; but after this decay set in and continued irresistibly throughout the period of the Medici grand dukes. Meanwhile, however, a great expansion had occurred in the Florentine silk industry. Prior to 1400 this had been of slight importance; but from the early years of the fifteenth century the demand for raw silk increased so rapidly, that foreign supplies, imported through Venice and Porto Pisano, no longer proved sufficient, and mulberry-growing and silkworm-breeding were locally developed, together with a rural industry of silk-throwing. Florentine exports of silken cloth rose steadily, especially during the sixteenth century. They were sold in all the principal centres of the Mediterranean and France, but their most important market was Lyons, where merchants of Florence and Lucca virtually controlled the trade for most of the sixteenth century.

In all the great commercial towns of Italy, the Mediterranean, and western Europe, the Florentines were still to be found in large numbers, as exporters of silks and woollens, dealers in miscellaneous merchandise, and most of all as bankers. And their international position was certainly as important as it had been in the early fourteenth century. But in relation to Florence itself, their situation had profoundly changed. Many Florentines were now dissuaded, for political or economic reasons, from ever returning home. For a time, it is true, they continued to maintain a regular business association with their native city, even after settling in Lyons, Paris, or Antwerp, but sooner or later the links were relaxed or broken; and for Florence this migration of wealthy merchants was an irreplaceable loss which contributed immensely to her economic decline.

4. THE PREDOMINANTLY AGRICULTURAL AREAS OF ITALY

No sharp distinction can be drawn, even in the age of the communes, between an industrial Italy and an agricultural Italy. Even in the most industrialized parts of the country the majority of people continued to work on the land. It is possible, however, to distinguish certain regions which were normally unable to grow enough food for the urban population and had to rely on imported produce, from others which grew a surplus of food but largely relied on imported manufactures. This difference was further deepened by the fact that the inhabitants of agricultural Italy rarely took an active part in external trade or even concerned themselves with the export of their own local produce. This passive attitude to trade was not confined to the south, but was common to all areas in which great centres of commerce and industry had failed to develop. Piedmont is a good example. During the Middle Ages parts of Piedmont were strongly influenced by the communal movement, and several important towns grew up, such as Asti, Chieri, Pinerolo, and

Biella, which were famous for their industries or for the activity of their merchants and moneylenders in countries abroad. But in the sixteenth century Piedmont was almost wholly agricultural, and its import and export trade was monopolized by merchants from outside, in particular Genoese. Similarly, in other regions of limited urban development, towns assumed a very different form from the greater communes of the middle and lower Po valley, Liguria, and Tuscany. Thus a number of small towns, especially in Romagna, Umbria, and the Marches, enjoyed a brief moment of splendour as the seat of petty princes, whose income from land, at home and elsewhere, and even more from their service as *condottieri* in the pay of the richest states in Italy, gave them a command of revenues far exceeding the economic capacity of the territories they ruled.

The unification of the Papal States, begun by cardinal Albornoz in the fourteenth century and then resumed with more lasting success by pope Julius II in the early sixteenth century, slowly destroyed the inflated prosperity of these tiny princely towns, but at the same time it stimulated the revival of the capital. From the beginning of the sixteenth century Rome recovered its ancient magnificence and resumed its place among the cosmopolitan cities of Europe. It was during the pontificate of Julius II that the great work of planning and rebuilding was launched, which was destined in the course of the next two centuries to create a new Rome, the Rome of the popes, with its monumental palaces and churches, fountains and squares. Within less than a hundred years, the population of the capital, which had sunk to a mere 30,000 souls at the end of the fifteenth century, was increased to 140,000 by a large and steady influx of new inhabitants. These immigrants included not only working people, but also ecclesiastics and officials, business men, artists, and writers, for whom papal Rome, from the time of Nicholas V and Pius II to the end of the sixteenth century, offered the most attractive opportunities of employment.

Inevitably the process of rapid growth and reconstruction made sixteenth-century Rome a busy market for consumer goods and a vigorous centre of production and exchange. But even so, both industry and trade—with the solitary exception of jewel-making—remained entirely local in scale and activity. The bank business, which throve to great importance in the service of the Roman Church and the expanding traffic of the city, was still largely controlled by foreigners or men of foreign origin, like the Spannocchi and Chigi of Siena, the Pazzi, Medici, and Altoviti of Florence, and the Welser and Fugger of Augsburg. There was no native aristocracy of money at this time. The great noble houses of Rome, and those which came to Rome from other parts of the Papal States, were either landowning families of feudal origin, endowed with vast estates in the neighbouring countryside from the Pontine Marshes and the Alban Hills to the territory of Viterbo, or families which owed a large part of their wealth and influence to the elevation of one of their members to an eminent position in the Church.

Very similar to Rome in economic and demographic development was another capital city, Naples, which grew so rapidly during the first half of the sixteenth century that it became not only the largest city in Italy, but also probably the largest city in Europe, excepting only Paris. The increase of population may not have been so sharp as would appear from certain official statistics, which indicate a rise from 40,000 souls in 1505 to 212,105 in 1547. The second of these figures, taken from a census made in time of famine for the distribution of bread, is almost certainly correct, whereas the 8,000 households assessed in 1505 for the distribution of salt probably represented only the taxpaying community. But there is no doubt whatever that, between these two dates, the urban population grew enormously, partly by the process of natural increase, but mainly by immigration. One stimulus to immigration was the policy of public works, begun by the viceroy Toledo; but the principal cause was the growing ascendancy of the capital in all departments of administrative, judicial, and social life throughout southern Italy, which inevitably drew to Naples not only large numbers of officials, but also an increasing proportion of the provincial nobility and scanty provincial middle class.

In spite, however, of this prodigious growth in size, Naples was no more destined than Rome to become a great industrial centre during this period. Some industries certainly flourished, such as the building industry, which created a heavy demand for labour, and a large number of small domestic and artisan crafts, which produced for local consumption. But, apart from the products of a few luxury industries, in particular the silk industry—which, despite government protection, never managed to absorb all the raw silk grown in the south—industrial output was so slight that Naples, in common with the rest of southern Italy, remained dependent on foreign producers for many manufactured goods, and offered tempting opportunities of investment for many foreign merchants and capitalists. Ever since the Angevin period, Naples had possessed a Genoese quarter, a Florentine quarter, and a Catalan quarter; and in the sixteenth century, Tuscans, Venetians, and still more Genoese, together with representatives of the big business houses of upper Germany, all retained a privileged position in the city, both as merchants and even more as bankers.

To be sure, there were a few small towns in the Papal States and the kingdom of Naples which maintained some independence of economic life and enterprise. Civitavecchia, for example, which the popes of the sixteenth century adopted as a naval base, had already grown to some importance earlier, as a port of exit for the alum of Tolfa and the timber and agricultural produce of the Maremma, and as a place of disembarkation for goods and persons bound for Rome. On the opposite coast lay Ancona, which although in partial decline since the loss of its full autonomy, was still the only Italian port on the Adriatic seaboard completely free of Venetian control. Indeed, during the sixteenth century, when the Ottoman fleet made conditions unsafe for maritime trade in the Aegean, Ancona acquired a certain importance as the port of embarkation for all those merchants travelling east, who preferred to go no further by sea than Spalato or Ragusa and then to proceed by land to Salonica, Constantinople, and the Black Sea ports.

A number of minor industries also prospered in the Papal States. The paper mills of Fabriano, Pioraco, and many other tiny towns of the Marches were celebrated for their products far outside Italy. The woollen cloth of Matelica was exported in quantity to neighbouring towns in the Marches and to the opposite shore of the Adriatic. The ceramics of Romagna, the

Marches, and Umbria brought world-wide fame to the artists of Faenza, Pesaro, Urbino, and Deruta.

In the kingdom of Naples it is difficult to speak of town life at all, in the economic sense of the term, outside the capital itself. A partial exception can be made, however, for a few coastal cities of Apulia, which took a share in Adriatic trade, for Gaeta on the Tyrrhenian seaboard, and for the inland towns of Benevento and Aquila, the second of which particularly was widely known during several centuries as a centre for the production and export of saffron.

In Sicily only one town, Messina, with its busy port and lively export trade in silk, still possesed a definite middle class in early modern times, or managed to preserve its ancient privileges intact.

This almost total absence of true towns and cities, to serve as centres of industry and trade, also influenced agriculture. In the writings of Renaissance authors, especially those devoted to the family and domestic economy, agriculture is invariably praised as the highest and most worthy of human occupations. But this deference to farming was mostly conventional, and must normally be treated, like the frequent translations of the Roman tracts on husbandry and other similar works, partly based on Roman models and partly on original observation, as expressing nothing more than the fashionable nostalgia for classical antiquity. As far as we can tell at least, the love for country manners hardly ever inspired a more practical love for country life, which might have induced the great landowners of the agricultural provinces of Italy to reside on their estates and dedicate their energy and capital to improving the land. On the contrary, it was precisely at this time that the landlords of Lazio and southern Italy surrendered most readily to the attractions of the capital and abandoned their properties to the care of managers, who were commonly peasants as ignorant and brutish as the rustics in their charge.

In those places where population was more dense and the neighbourhood of a market or port encouraged trade, we find the land minutely divided and intensively cultivated by small-holders and emphyteutic tenants, who chose to raise the crops most suitable for local sale. Such districts were the Terra di

Lavoro and the country round Vesuvius, the Sorrentine peninsula, the south and east coasts of Sicily, the southernmost point
of Calabria, a few short stretches of coastal Apulia, and the
Alban Hills. But outside these isolated areas the land was
dominated by great estates, which were ill adapted to technical
innovation and were destined, in fact, to perpetuate for centuries the most ancient systems of husbandry. If, in spite of this
stagnation, the inland parts of Sicily and vast tracts of Apulia
and the Roman and Tuscan Maremma could still export large
quantities of corn during the Renaissance period to Florence,
Genoa, and Venice, the reason, as we have said, was not the
high level of production but the low density of population and
the even lower standard of living.

The low level of population, and also partly the arid conditions prevailing in large areas of the south, go far to explain
the great development of sheep-farming, which during the
Aragonese period was reorganized, in the Tavoliere di Apulia,
upon principles largely new to Italy, if not unknown to Spain.
One of the first acts of King Alfonso of Aragon was to improve
southern stock-raising by introducing the highly valued breed
of merino sheep, and to impose controls on the primordial
custom of transhumance between the summer grazings of the
Abruzzi and the winter grazings of the Apulian plain, by
reserving the greater part of the Tavoliere exclusively to
pasture. The famous "Customs organization for migrant sheep"
(*Dogana della mena delle pecore*), which Alfonso founded in
imitation of age-long practice on the highland pastures of
Spain, not only enriched the Crown with new revenue; it also
gave a powerful impetus to the production of wool, so that
Foggia became for several centuries the most important wool
market in Italy.

But this development was exceptional. It was also confined to
a branch of husbandry, sheep-rearing, which normally prospers
in underdeveloped regions, or in countries condemned for
reasons of climate and population to remain largely unculti-
vated. One obvious feature of southern Italy, Sicily, and much
of the Papal States, was the deep division existing between the
coastal areas and the interior. Even today, centuries of history
seem to separate Rome from the communities of the Ciociaria,
Naples from the townships of the Molise and Basilicata,

Catania from Enna; their mutual isolation was far more complete in the later Middle Ages, when the hinterland could only be reached on mule-back, in the face of difficulties, discomforts, and dangers of every kind. If therefore, in certain favoured districts of Italy, even southern Italy, we find evidence of a changing world, where agriculture was becoming commercialized, trade attracted merchants from all directions, and the economy was in the fullest sense an economy of exchange, in other regions—which unfortunately made up the greater if not the more populous part of the country—there was not the slightest stir of innovation, the economy was still mainly a natural economy, and the peasant population was kept in utter subjection to a class of feudal magnates. So it remained in much of the south down to the Bourbon period, and the vestiges have not yet vanished today.

Bibliographical Note

The most recent GENERAL WORKS ON THE ECONOMIC HISTORY OF MEDIEVAL ITALY are: A. Doren, *Wirtschaftsgeschichte Italiens im Mittelalter* (Jena, 1934; Ital. trans., with amendments, by G. Luzzatto, Padua, 1937), and G. Luzzatto, *Storia economica d'Italia*, vol. I, *L'antichità e il Medio Evo* (Rome, 1949; revised edition of the medieval part announced). The only surveys in English are the chapters by G. Mickwitz on agrarian Italy, in the *Cambridge Economic History*, vol. I (Cambridge, 1942), by R. S. Lopez on Mediterranean trade, in *Camb. Ec. Hist.* vol. II (1952), and by C. Cipolla on finance, etc., in *Camb. Ec. Hist.* vol. III (1960); a revised version of the chapter on agrarian Italy, by P. J. Jones, will appear in the second edition of *Camb. Ec. Hist.* vol. I. All these chapters have an extensive bibliography. The commercial history of medieval Italy is amply illustrated in the volume: *Medieval trade in the Mediterranean world*, ed. R. S. Lopez, I. W. Raymond (O.U.P., 1955), a collection of documents in translation, with commentary. New work may be followed in the journal *Economia e Storia* (1954 ff.), of which the number for 1958 contains a bibliographical survey of Italian economic history by M. R. Caroselli.

On the DECLINE OF ROMAN ITALY see: M. I. Rostovtzeff, *The social and economic history of the Roman Empire* (2nd ed., Oxford, 1957), C. E. Stevens, "Agriculture and rural life in the later Roman Empire", *Camb. Ec. Hist.* vol. I, F. W. Walbank, "Trade and industry under the later Roman Empire in the west", *Camb. Ec. Hist.* vol. II, A. H. M. Jones, *Ancient Economic History* (London, 1948) and "The decline and fall of the Roman Empire", *History*, 1955.

The GERMANIC INVASIONS and the division of Italy between Lombards and Byzantines can still be usefully studied in: T. Hodgkin, *Italy and her invaders* (2nd ed., Oxford, 1892 ff.). The standard histories are: L. M. Hartmann, *Geschichte Italiens im Mittelalter* (Gotha, 1897 ff.), and G. Romano, *Le dominazioni barbariche* (Milan, 1909, partially revised by A. Solmi, 1940). For a lively summary see also: G. Pepe, *Il Medio Evo barbarico d'Italia* (Turin, 1942; French trans., Paris, 1956). Indispensable for the economic history of this period are also: A. Dopsch, *The economic and social foundations of European civilization* (London, 1937), and H. Pirenne, *Mohammed and Charlemagne* (New York, 1939), on which cp. A. Riising, "The fate of Henri Pirenne's theses", *Classica et Medievalia*, 1952, and R. S. Lopez,

Bibliographical Note

"East and west in the early Middle Ages", *X Congresso internaz. di scienze storiche, Relazioni* III (1955).

More specifically on LOMBARD SETTLEMENT AND SOCIETY see: E. Besta, *Storia del diritto italiano. Diritto pubblico* (Milan, 1941), G. P. Bognetti, in *S. Maria di Castelseprio* (Milan, 1948), and in vol. II of *Storia di Milano* (Fondazione Treccani, Milan, 1954); on the LATE LOMBARD AND EARLY CAROLINGIAN ECONOMY see: L. M. Hartmann, *Zur Wirtschaftsgeschichte Italiens im frühen Mittelalter, Analekten* (Gotha, 1904), G. Volpe's review of this in his volume, *Medio Evo Italiano* (Florence, 1923), and F. Carli, *Il mercato nell'alto Medio Evo*, vol. I (Padua, 1931); on TRADE IN BYZANTINE ITALY see: A. Schaube, *Handelsgeschichte der romanischen Völker des Mittelmeergebiets bis zum Ende der Kreuzzüge* (Munich, 1906; Ital. trans., Turin, 1915), A. R. Lewis, *Naval power and trade in the Mediterranean, A.D. 500–1100* (Princeton, 1951); on the ECONOMIC ORGANIZATION OF THE GREAT ESTATES see: T. Mommsen, "Die Bewirtschaftung der Kirchengüter unter Gregor I", *Zeitschrift für Sozial- und Wirtschaftsgeschichte*, 1893, G. Seregni, "La popolazione agricola della Lombardia nell'età barbarica", *Archivio storica lombardo*, 1895, Hartmann, *Analekten cit.*, G. Luzzatto, *I servi nelle grandi proprietà ecclesiastiche dei secoli IX e X* (Pisa, 1910); on LOMBARD COINAGE AND THE LATE LOMBARD ECONOMIC REVIVAL see: U. Monneret de Villard, "La moneta in Italia nell'alto Medio Evo", *Rivista italiana di numismatica*, 1919, P. Grierson, "The silver coinage of the Lombards", *Archivio storico lombardo*, 1957, and Carli, *Mercato cit.*; and on the ORIGINS OF VENICE see: R. Cessi, *Venezia ducale*, vol. I (Venice, 1940), L. M. Hartmann, in *Vierteljahrschrift für Sozial und Wirtschaftsgeschichte*, 1905, and G. Luzzatto, "Les activités économiques du patriciat vénitien", *Annales d'histoire économique et sociale*, 1937.

Fundamental for the GENERAL HISTORY OF FEUDALISM are: M. Bloch, *Feudal Society* (London, 1961), and C. A. Mor, *L'età feudale* (Milan, 1952); on FEUDALISM AND THE GREAT ESTATES, and THE BEGINNINGS OF SOCIAL CHANGE IN TOWN AND COUNTRY, see particularly: P. S. Leicht, *Studi sulla proprietà in Italia*, vol. I (Padua, 1903), F. Schneider, *Die Entstehung v. Burg u. Landgemeinde in Italien* (Berlin, 1924), C. Violante, *La società milanese nell'età precomunale* (Naples, 1954).

For the MARITIME TOWNS BETWEEN THE NINTH AND ELEVENTH CENTURIES see: Schaube, *op. cit.*, Lewis, *op. cit.*; C. Manfroni, *Storia della marina italiana* (Leghorn, 1899), G. Coniglio, "Amalfi e il commercio amalfitano" etc., *Nuova rivista storica*, 1944–5, M. Merores, *Gaeta im frühen Mittelalter* (Gotha, 1911), G. Padovan (pseudonym of G. Luzzatto), "Capitale e lavoro nel commercio veneziano dei secoli XI e XII", *Rivista di storia economica*, 1941 (reprinted in his *Studi di storia economica veneziana*, Padua, 1955), G. Volpe, *Studi sulle istituzioni comunali a Pisa nei secoli XII e XIII* (Pisa, 1902), R. S. Lopez, "Aux origines du capitalisme génois", *Annales d'histoire économique et sociale*, 1937. For PAVIA AND NORTHERN ITALY see especially: A. Solmi, *L'amministrazione finanziaria del regno italico nell'alto Medio Evo* (Pavia, 1932).

The ECONOMIC AND SOCIAL HISTORY OF THE EARLY COMMUNES is dispersed in numberless local monographs, and up-to-date synopses are few (outside the general histories listed above). Of special interest are the two studies by G. Volpe, "Questioni fondamentali sull' origine e svolgimento dei communi italiani", and "Una nuova teoria sulle origini del comune", both reprinted in his *Medio Evo Italiano cit.* The chapter by Previté-Orton in the *Cambridge Medieval History*, vol. V (1926), may also be consulted, and the brief collection of documents by P. Brezzi, *I comuni cittadini italiani* (Milan, 1940). For southern Italy see: F. Calasso, *La legislazione statutaria dell'Italia meridionale* (Rome, 1929).

On ITALIAN TRADE AND COLONIZATION IN THE MEDITERRANEAN during and after the Crusades see particularly: W. Heyd, *Histoire du commerce du Levant au Moyen-Age* (Leipzig, 1885), R. Cessi, *Le colonie medievali italiane in Oriente* (Padua, 1942), H. Brown, "The Venetians and the Venetian quarter in Constantinople", *Journal of Hellenic Studies*, 1920, G. I. Bratianu, *Les Vénitiens dans la Mer Noire au XIVe siècle* (Bucarest, 1939), H. Sieveking, *Genueser Finanzwesen* (Frieburg-i.-B., 1898, Tübingen, 1900; partial Ital. trans., in *Atti Società Storia Patria per la Liguria*, 1906–7), E. H. Byrne, "Genoese trade with Syria in the twelfth century", *American Historical Review*, 1920, "The Genoese colonies in Syria", *Historical essays presented to D. C. Munro* (New York, 1928), R. S. Lopez, *Storia delle colonie genovesi nel Mediterraneo* (Bologna, 1938), G. I. Bratianu, *Recherches sur le commerce génois dans la Mer Noire au XIIIe siècle* (Paris, 1929), E. Rossi-Sabatini, *L'espansione di Pisa nel Mediterraneo* (Florence, 1935), G. M. Monti, *L'espansione mediterranea del Mezzogiorno d'Italia e della Sicilia* (Bologna, 1942), L. Olschki, *Marco Polo's precursors* (Baltimore, 1943).

On the interrelated questions of URBAN IMMIGRATION, TOWN AND COUNTRY, AND CHANGES IN RURAL STATUS AND TENURE, see: R. Caggese, "La repubblica di Siena e il suo contado nel secolo xiii", *Bollettino senese di storia patria*, 1906, G. Luzzatto, "Le sottomissioni dei feudatari e le classi sociali in alcuni comuni marchigiani", *Le Marche*, 1906, G. De Vergottini, *Origini e sviluppo della comitatinanza*, Siena, 1929, J. Plesner, *L'émigration de la campagne à la ville de Florence au XIIIe siècle* (Copenhagen, 1934), G. Luzzatto, "L'inurbamento delle popolazioni rurali in Italia nei secoli XII e XIII", in *Studi di storia e di diritto in onore di E. Besta* (Milan, 1938), E. Fiumi, "Sui rapporti economici tra città e contado nell' età communale", *Archivio storico italiano* 1956, R. Pöhlmann, *Die Wirtschaftspolitik der Florentiner Renaissance* (Leipzig, 1878), P. Vaccari, *L'affrancazione dei servi nell'Emilia e nella Toscana* (Bologna, 1926), P. J. Jones, "An Italian estate, 900–1200", *Economic History Review*, 1954, "A Tuscan monastic lordship in the later Middle Ages: Camaldoli", *Journal of Ecclesi-*

Bibliographical Note

astical History, 1954, I. Imberciadori, *Mezzadria classica toscana* (Florence) 1951).

The FOOD POLICY of the communes is reviewed by H. C. Peyer, *Zur Getreidepolitik oberitalienischen Städte im XIII Jahrhundert* (Vienna, 1950). On the GUILDS, AND THE ECONOMIC POLICY OF THE COMMUNES, see: G. Arias, *Il sistema della costituzione economica e sociale italiana nell'età die comuni* (Turin–Rome, 1906), on which compare the searching review by G. Volpe in his *Medio Evo italiano cit.*; F. Valsecchi, *Le corporazioni nell'organismo politico del Medio Evo* (Milan, 1931), with full bibliography.

The ECONOMIC AND SOCIAL DEVELOPMENT OF THE COMMUNES IN THE THIRTEENTH AND FOURTEENTH CENTURIES is mainly described, like their earlier history, in regional monographs. Two useful works of a general nature are: G. Fasoli, "La legislazione antimagnatizia dei comuni dell' alta e media Italia", *Rivista di storia del diritto italiano*, 1939, G. De Vergottini, *Arti e popolo nella prima metà del secolo XIII* (Milan, 1943). Cp. also: G. Salvemini, *Magnati e popolani in Firenze dal 1280 al 1295* (Florence, 1899 reprinted, without the valuable appendices, Turin, 1960), F. Schevill, *History of Florence* (New York, 1936), N. Ottokar, *Il comune di Firenze alla fine del Dugento* (Florence, 1926), N. Rodolico, "The struggle for the right of association in fourteenth-century Florence", *History*, 1922, *I Ciompi, Una pagina della storia del proletariate operaio* (Florence, 1945), D. Herlihy, *Pisa in the early Renaissance* (Yale Univ. Press, 1958).

The only history of MEDIEVAL ITALIAN AGRICULTURE remains the brief sketch of G. Bertagnolli, *Delle vicende dell'agricoltura in Italia* (Florence, 1881). For further details cp. A. Gloria, *Dell'agricoltura nel Padovano* (Padua, 1855), F. Gabotto, *L'agricoltura nella regione saluzzese dal secolo XI al XV* (Turin, 1901), A. Lizier, *L'economia rurale dell'età prenormanna nell' Italia meridionale* (Palermo, 1907), P. Torelli, *Un comune cittadino in territorio ad economia agricola* (Mantua, 1930), L. Messedaglia, *Per la storia dell'agricoltura e dell'alimentazione* (Piacenza, 1932). There is no modern edition, though many old editions, of Pietro de' Crescenzi.

On the MINING INDUSTRY see: C. Baudi de Vesme, *Dell'industria delle miniere nel territorio di Villa di Chiesa* (Turin, 1870), G. Volpe, "Montieri", *Vierteljahrschrift für Sozial u. Wirtschaftsgeschichte*, 1908, R. S. Lopez, "Contributo alla storia delle miniere argentifere della Sardegna", in *Studi economico-giuridici della R. Università di Cagliari*, 1936; on ARMAMENTS: A. Schulte, *Geschichte des mittelalterlichen Handels u. Verkehrs zwischen Westdeutschland u. Italien* (Leipzig, 1900); on SHIPBUILDING: Manfroni, *op. cit.*, G. Luzzatto, "Per la storia delle costruzioni navali", in *Miscellanea Manfroni* (Venice, 1925), F. C. Lane, *Venetian ships and shipbuilding* (Baltimore, 1934); on COTTON MANUFACTURE: F. Borlandi, "Futainiers et futaines dans l'Italie du Moyen Age" in *Hommage à Lucien Febvre II* (Paris, 1953); on SILK: R. Broglio d'Aiano, *L'arte della seta in Venezia*

Bibliographical Note

(Milan, 1902), P. Pieri, "Intorno alla storia dell' arte della seta a Firenze", *Archivio storico italiano*, 1927, N. Dorini, *L'arte della seta in Toscana* (Florence, 1928), E. Lazzareschi, *L'arte della seta in Lucca* (Lucca, 1930), H. Sieveking, "Die genueser Seidenindustrie in XIV Jahrhundert", *Jahrbuch für Gesetzgebung*, 1897; on WOOL: E. Carus-Wilson, "The woollen industry", *Camb. Ec. Hist.*, vol. II (with full bibliography).

The main source for studying THE RANGE OF ITALIAN COMMERCE about 1300 is Francesco Pegolotti's handbook, *La pratica della mercatura*, ed. A. Evans (Cambridge, Mass., 1936), on which cp. P. Grierson, "The coin list of Pegolotti", *Studi in onore di A. Sapori* (Milan, 1957).

For TRANSPORT BY LAND see: Schulte, *op. cit.*, A. Schaube, "Die Kuriendienst zwischen Italien u. den Messen v. Champagne", *Archiv f. Post u. Telegraph*, 1896, J. T. Tyler, *The Alpine passes in the Middle Ages* (Oxford, 1930), I. Renouard, "Comment les papes d'Avignon expédiaient leur courier", *Revue historique*, 1937; on the COST OF LAND TRANSPORT: Schulte, *op. cit.*, A. Sapori, *Una compagnia di Calimala ai primi del Trecento* (Florence, 1932), A. Fanfani, "Costi e profitti di Lazzaro Bracco mercante aretino del Trecento", in his *Saggi di storia economica italiana* (Milan, 1936), C. Cipolla, in *Bollettino storico pavese*, 1944; on RIVER TRANSPORT see: G. Biscaro, "Gli antichi navigli milanesi", *Archivio storico lombardo*, 1908, A. Solmi, "Le diete imperiali di Roncaglia e la navigazione del Po presso Piacenza", *Bollettino della soc. di storia patria per le prov. parmensi*, 1910; on TRANSPORT AND TRADE BY SEA: K. Kretschmer, *Die italienischen portolani des Mittelalters* (Berlin, 1909), R. Predelli and A. Sacerdoti, "Gli statuti marittimi veneziani fino al 1255", *Nuovo archivio veneto*, 1902, G. Yver, *Le commerce et les marchands dans l'Italie méridionale au XIIIe et au XIVe siècle* (Paris, 1903), A. Schaube 'Die Anfänge der venetianischen Galeerenfahrten nach den Nordsee", *Historische Zeitschrift*, 1908, R. Cessi, "Le relazioni commerciali tra Venezia e le Fiandre nel secolo XIV", *N. Archivo Veneto*, 1914, R. Doehaerd, "Les galères génoises dans la Manche et la Mer du Nord à la fin du XIIIe et au début du XIVe siècle", *Bulletin de l'Institut historique belge de Rome*, 1938, E. H. Byrne, *Genoese shipping in the twelfth and thirteenth centuries* (Cambridge, Mass., 1930), A. Grunzweig, "Les fonds du consulat de la mer aux archives de l'Etat à Florence", *Bulletin belge cit.* 1930; for COSTS OF SEA TRANSPORT cp. F. Melis, "La formazione dei costi nell'industria laniera", *Economia e storia*, 1954.

The most comprehensive study of ITALIAN MERCHANTS IN THE MIDDLE AGES is by A. Sapori, *Le marchand italien au Moyen Age* (Paris, 1952, with ample bibliography). No less valuable are his other works: *La crisi delle compagnie mercantili dei Bardi e dei Peruzzi* (Florence 1926), *Una compagnia di Calimala cit.*, and his *Studi di storia economica medievale* (3rd ed., Florence, 1955). Cp. also L. Zdekauer, *Il mercante senese nel Duecento* (Siena, 1901), and in English: G. Niccolini di Camugliano, *The chronicles of a Florentine family 1200–1470* (London, 1933), F. C. Lane, *Andrea Barbarigo,*

Bibliographical Note

merchant of Venice, 1418–1449 (Baltimore 1944). (Little can be said for the popular life of Francesco Datini by I. Origo (*Merchant of Prato*, London, 1957), which, despite pretensions to exact and original scholarship, is mostly unoriginal and sadly inexact: see F. Melis, in *Economia e Storia* vi (1959), 737 ff.)

For the history of COMMERCIAL CONTRACTS AND PART-NERSHIPS see in particular: L. Goldschmidt, *Universalgeschichte des Handelsrechts* (Stuttgart, 1891; Ital. trans., Turin, 1913), G. Artusi, *Origini e svolgimento storico della commenda fino al secolo XIII* (Turin, 1933), G. Luzzatto, " La commenda nella vita economica dei secoli XIII e XIV con particolare riguardo a Venezia", *Atti del convegno di Amalfi* (Naples, 1934), and the works of Sapori listed above.

Most studies of PUBLIC FINANCE are regional or local. Especially useful are: H. Sieveking, *Genueser Finanzwesen cit.*, B. Barbadoro, *Le finanze della repubblica fiorentina* (Florence, 1929), G. Biscaro, "Gli estimi del comune di Milano nel secolo XIII", *Archivio storico lombardo*, 1928, E. Fiumi, "L'imposta ·diretta nei comuni medioevali della Toscana", *Studi in onore d. A. Sapori* (Milan, 1957). See also the *Documenti finanziari della repubblica veneta*, in particular: *Bilanci generali* (ed. F. Besta, Venice, 1912), *La regolazione delle entrate e delle spese* (ed. R. Cessi, Padua, 1925), and *I prestiti della repubblica di Venezia nei secoli XIII–XIV* (ed. G. Luzzatto, Padua, 1929).

On COINAGE AND MONETARY POLICY see: C. M. Cipolla, *Money, prices and civilization in the Mediterranean world, fifth to seventeenth centuries* (Princeton, 1956). R. S. Lopez, "An aristocracy of money in the early Middle Ages", *Speculum*, 1953, and "Back to gold, 1252", *Economic history review*, 1956–7, 219 ff. (cp. P. Grierson, *ibid.* 462 ff.); D. Herlihy, "Pisan coinage and the monetary development of Tuscany, 1150–1250", *American numismatic society, Museum notes*, 1954. R. Cessi, "Studi sulla moneta veneziana", *Economia*, 1924–5, C. M. Cipolla, *Studi di storia della moneta. I I movimenti dei cambi in Italia dal secolo XIII al XV* (Pavia, 1948).

On BANKING see: articles by Luzzatto and Sieveking, in J. G. Van Dillen, *Contributions to the history of banking* (The Hague, 1934), A. P. Usher, *The early history of deposit banking* (Harvard Univ. Press, 1943), R. De Roover, *Money, banking and credit in medieval Bruges* (Cambridge, Mass., 1948), *The Medici Bank* (New York, 1948).

On the BILL OF EXCHANGE see: R. De Roover, *L'évolution de la lettre de change, XIVe–XVIIIe siècle* (Paris 1953); and on ACCOUNTING: the articles by Florence Edler De Roover, R. De Roover, and R. Emmett Taylor, in *Studies in the history of accounting*, ed. A. C. Littleton, B. S. Yamey (London, 1956).

The ECONOMIC HISTORY OF RENAISSANCE ITALY awaits systematic study. For some points of view see C. M. Cipolla, "The trends in Italian economic history in the later Middle Ages", *Economic History Review*, 1949–50, and his chapter in the *Storia di Milano*, vol. VII

(Foundazione Treccani, Milan, 1957); R. S. Lopez, "Hard times and investment in culture", in *The Renaissance. A Symposium* (New York, 1953), and his debate with H. Baron in *American Historical Review*, 1956 (all now excerpted in *The Renaissance, Medieval or Modern?*, ed. K. H. Dannenfeldt, Boston, Mass., 1959); P. J. Jones, "Florentine families and Florentine diaries of the fourteenth century", *Papers of the British School in Rome*, 1956.

Index

Index

Index

Transport, *see* Communications
Trebizond, 87
Trentino, 102, 103, 115
Treviso, 28, 35, 36
Turks, 76, 138, 141, 145, 147, 150, 164
Tuscany, 12, 18, 19, 32, 37, 55, 76, 79, 89, 90, 94, 95 ff., 101, 102, 103, 104, 111, 115, 121, 139, 156, 158 ff., 166

Umbria, 18, 162, 165

Vendramin, Andrea, 153–4
Venetia, 18, 27, 39, 95, 104, 106, 134, 139, 142
Venice, 28, 32 ff., 49, 50, 51 ff., 59, 72, 73 ff., 76 ff., 86 ff., 91, 96, 97, 105, 106, 107, 110, 111, 112,

113, 115, 118, 119, 121, 122, 123, 124–6, 127, 128–9, 130–1, 132, 133, 139, 140, 141, 142, 145, 146–7, 150 ff., 160, 164, 166
Vercelli, 6, 58
Verona, 15, 27, 28, 58, 95, 99, 102, 115, 117, 139
Via Emilia, 95, 96
Via Francigena, 54, 58, 95, 96
Villani, Giovanni, 97, 106, 114
Visigoths, 11
Vivaldi, the brothers, 139
Volterra, 27
Voyages of discovery, 138, 139–40, 148

Wages, 129 ff.
Welser, the, 163

180